Let's Cook!

T0044717

Susan McQuillan, RD

HOUGHTON MIFFLIN HARCOURT

BOSTON • NEW YORK

Contributing Writer and Editor Leslie A. Kimmelman

Sesame Workshop
Vice President, Worldwide Publishing Jennifer A. Perry
Health and Education Consultant Jane Park Woo

Houghton Mifflin Harcourt
Vice President and Publisher Natalie Chapman
Executive Editor Linda Ingroia
Art Director Tai Blanche
Managing Editor Marina Padakis Lowry
Production Editor Jamie Selzer
Production Director Tom Hyland

Photographer Lucy Schaeffer
Food Stylist Claudia Ficca
Prop Stylist Margaret Ward

"Sesame Workshop"®, "Sesame Street"®, and associated characters, trademarks, and design elements are owned and licensed by Sesame Workshop.
© 2015 Sesame Workshop. All rights reserved.

Food photography © 2014 by Sesame Workshop
All rights reserved.

For information about permission to reproduce selections from this book, write to trade.permissions@hmhco.com or to Permissions, Houghton Mifflin Harcourt Publishing Company, 3 Park Avenue, 19th Floor, New York, New York 10016.

www.hmhco.com

Library of Congress Cataloging-in-Publication Data is available upon request.
ISBN 978-0-544-45436-1(hardcover); ISBN 978-0-544-45366-1 (ebk)
Printed in China
SCP 15 14 13 12 11 10 9 8
4500812140

This cookbook is dedicated to my taster-in-chief,
Molly McQuillan, with special thanks to Isabel Schnock, Ruby Serafin,
Phebe McManamon, and Owen McManamon
for recipe testing and tasting and for contributing great ideas.

Contents

Introduction

The goal of *Let's Cook!* is to bring adults and young children together in the kitchen to create tasty, healthful food for the entire family to enjoy. While children help with the cooking, they will be learning about different kinds of foods and different ways to prepare them; they will be developing healthy eating habits; and they will be boosting their understanding of nutrition, math, language skills, science, diversity, and cultural awareness. The more time your children spend helping you with meal preparation—from food shopping to serving the meal—the more curious and open-minded they will become about their own food choices. And for the kids, what's the icing on the cake, so to speak? They get to have fun with their friends—the happy, healthy monsters of *Sesame Street*!

While you are teaching your children to prepare and cook food—with the help of Elmo, Cookie Monster, Grover, Big Bird, Rosita, Abby Cadabby, and the rest of the gang—you can also teach them about cleaning up after themselves. You may be surprised to find that children actually enjoy their kitchen cleanup chores. It's just another way they can contribute to the family meal.

It may get messy, but having young children help prepare meals and snacks from scratch provides benefits that reach well beyond your kitchen. It builds a foundation for making smart food choices as they grow into adolescents and young adults. As they grow up, they can enhance the basic skills and knowledge they acquired and become more self-sufficient. There are rewards for adults as well. As your children get older, they will become a true help to you in the kitchen. Someday they may be the chefs, and you the assistant!

Perhaps the most satisfying immediate result of cooking with young children is seeing them beam with pride as they share the food they helped to make with family and friends. Cooking with children is as much about sharing family time and creating memories as it is about learning new skills and developing a positive attitude and an interest in trying new foods.

Notes on the recipes

The recipes in this book are written for you, the adult, to help you prepare healthful meals with and for your family. They have been developed to be flexible so that you (and your children) can create dishes that suit the varying tastes and needs of different family members.

For instance, **Chilly Outside? Elmo's Chili Inside!** (page 75) can be made with chicken, turkey, beef, or pork. Because the meat is cooked separately and added to the pot near the end of the chili cooking time, it can also be prepared as a vegetarian dish. Countless veggie combinations can be used to make **Oscar's Cream of Any-Old-Thing Leftover Soup** (page 43), **Grover's Asian Sticky Rice Balls** (page 63), or **Rosita's Veggie-Cheese Quesadillas** (page 51). A basic fruit smoothie can take on endless flavor possibilities simply by changing the type of yogurt or fruit you use. The **Pizza Party on Sesame Street!** (page 76) recipe makes enough dough for eight individual pies and allows everyone to custom design the toppings. And in **Grover's Gado-Gado** (page 72), just about anything you can think of eating is perfect for dipping into the tasty peanut sauce.

Every recipe in this book also includes at least one variation, either in the recipe itself or in how it is served. Fill **Zoe's Sweet and Special Birthday Cake** (page 122) with sweetened ricotta cream, or, if you don't wish to use ricotta cheese, you can substitute pureed banana. The fluffy homemade waffles in **Elmo's Waffle Sandwich Melt** (page 25) are topped with melted cheese, but they could be topped with juicy fresh fruit instead.

There are very simply seasoned dishes as well as more flavorful dishes that feature a variety of herbs as well as spices, including pepper, paprika, cayenne powder, ginger, and cinnamon, for the best-tasting dish without relying on too much salt or, in some cases, sugar. Children around the world grow up with these tasty seasonings from an early age. Of course, adjust the flavors to your family's preferences.

The recipes are written with full ingredient and equipment lists so you can be sure to have everything you need on hand before beginning to prep ingredients and equipment and cook. Your child can help you prepare to cook by collecting ingredients (such as produce or ingredients in small plastic containers) and utensils (such as spatulas, wooden spoons, and plastic bowls) that are safe for them to retrieve and carry to your kitchen work area.

Icons
KIDS!

Each of the 50 recipes in this book contains at least two steps that a child between the ages of two and five can safely and easily accomplish, depending on both the age and skill level of the individual child, and *always* with the supervision of an adult. This icon never suggests that a child can work alone on a step; an adult may have to help guide the child's hand or elaborate on the instructions.

PACK AND CARRY

You will see this icon whenever a recipe is suitable for packing and traveling. Some foods can travel in food-storage bags or covered containers while others, like soups and smoothies, can travel in a thermos. Any dish that normally requires refrigeration and won't be eaten within two hours will, of course, have to travel with an ice pack.

HAPPY HEALTHY MONSTER TIP

Many recipes have an icon like this. This tip will indicate key nutrition information as well as ideas on healthy eating.

A Word About Portion Sizes and Good Nutrition for Happy Healthy Monsters

The yield, or number of servings, noted on any recipe in this book is based on standard serving sizes, not on child-size portions. That means a four-serving dish might actually feed five or six people, depending on individual ages and appetites.

To help children stay healthy, keep offering a range of nutritious food choices for meals and snacks. Encourage them to eat their colors by having a colorful array of fruits and vegetables on the menu.

Enjoy mealtimes together as a family. This is a special time to connect and catch up on the news of the day. Eating as a family also helps children develop more positive attitudes about food and leads to healthier eating. Encourage your children to listen to their bodies. Teach them words like *hungry* and *full*. Start off with smaller portions of a variety of foods, and assure children they can have seconds if they are still hungry. This is good advice for grown-ups, too!

A Word About Food Allergies

Common allergens include peanuts and other nuts, fish, shellfish, eggs, milk and other dairy products, soy, and wheat. If allergies exist, be sure to carefully read the ingredient list on all food labels to avoid the offending food. Be especially careful with food products imported from other countries. Do not use any processed food products that do not display a complete list of ingredients.

Even if a product does not contain a food allergen, it may have been processed on equipment that also processes those common allergens. This information is normally printed just below the ingredients list on a food label. When a child has food allergies, he or she should not even be in the same room with any product that contains that allergen, as food particles can become airborne and be inhaled.

When you cook with or for other people's children, always double-check with their parents or guardians about possible food allergies or sensitivities. Note: Honey, which is included in several recipes here, should not be given to a child one year old or younger.

Kitchen Safety 1-2-3

REMEMBER! Children must be supervised in the kitchen at all times, even when they are performing age-appropriate tasks.

Here are the safety rules all happy healthy monsters follow in the kitchen. *Read them out loud with your child before you start to cook:*

1 Make sure there is a grown-up nearby whenever you're working in the kitchen.

2 Always ask a grown-up when you need help preparing food or if you can't reach something you need.

3 Grown-ups should create a special place for you to work in the kitchen. This place should be away from hot things like the stove and away from any pots, pans, appliances, or utensils that could fall on you and hurt you.

4 Never touch a knife, food processor blade, blender blade, scissors, or other sharp object in the kitchen.

5 If you have long hair, tie it back.

6 If you are wearing clothing with long sleeves, roll them up.

7 Always start with a clean kitchen. You can help a grown-up wipe off the counter and put away anything you don't need so that you have lots of space to work.

8 Ask a grown-up to read the recipe out loud before you start preparing food. Help the grown-up gather the food and equipment you need. When you are done with an ingredient, help a grown-up put away any leftovers. When you are done with equipment, help a grown-up put it aside to be cleaned. Make sure a grown-up is nearby when you cut soft foods, such as bananas or bread, with a plastic serrated knife. Ask that grown-up to show you how to cut away from your fingers so you don't get hurt.

9 Never go near a hot stove, oven, or waffle iron without a grown-up nearby. Grown-ups are responsible for putting food in the oven and taking it out, and for cooking food on top of the stove or in the waffle iron.

10 Help keep the kitchen safe. Remind grown-ups to make sure there are no pot handles sticking out from the stove and no wires hanging off the counter. Also, tell a grown-up if you see a knife or other sharp utensil lying around.

11 Work slowly and carefully, and do just one job at a time. Always ask a grown-up what to do next, before you do it!

A Word About Young Children and Choking

Young children are still learning to chew and swallow properly as their teeth develop and as they learn how to eat different types of food. All firm foods, such as many raw fruits and vegetables, dried fruit and other sticky foods, and nuts and other hard foods, must be cut into very small pieces or finely chopped or ground so they are safe for children to swallow. When everyone sits down at the table, it is important to eat slowly and chew food very well before swallowing it.

The ABCs of Healthy Foods

A GOOD-FOOD ALPHABET FOR YOUR *HAPPY HEALTHY MONSTER!*

These foods are really delicious—*and* they keep your body strong and healthy. Elmo wonders: How many of these foods have you seen at the market? Which ones have you tasted? What other foods can you think of that begin with the first letter of your name? What foods can you think of that begin with the other letters of the alphabet?

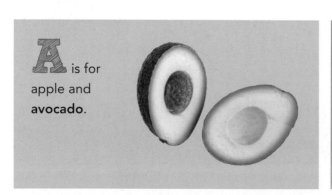

A is for apple and **avocado**.

B is for **beets** and broccoli.

C is for **chicken** and carrots.

G is for **garbanzo beans** and green beans.

D is for **dates** and dandelion greens.

H is for **honeydew melon**.

E is for **eggs**. It's also for eggplants, which are shaped like eggs (only larger!).

I is for **iceberg lettuce**.

F is for **fish**.

J is for **jicama** (say *HEE-ca-mah*). That's a Mexican root vegetable!

K is for **kiwi** and kale (and both of them are green!).

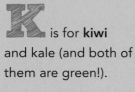

O is for **olives** and **olive oil**. Can you say *olio d'oliva* (*OH-lee-oh doh-LEE-vah*)? That's Italian for "olive oil"!

L is for **lentils**, which are part of the legume family.

P is for **plum** and peas.

M is for **mushrooms**.

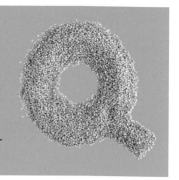

Q is for **quinoa** (say *KEEN-wah*). Quinoa is a healthy and delicious grain from South America.

N is for **nectarine**, nice and juicy.

R is for **rice**, which rhymes with nice!

S is for **sweet potato**. It's delicious stuffed!

W is for **watermelon**, which is sweet— and full of healthy water.

T is for **tomatoes** and turkey.

X is for *xiāngjiāo* (say *she-ang-GEE-ow*). That's how you say "banana" in Chinese!

U is for *uvas* (say *OO-vas*). That's Spanish for "grapes"!

Y is for **yogurt**. Yummy!

V is for **vegetables**. Can you find these veggies in the photo: carrots, corn, kale, and radishes?

Z is for (zingy) **zucchini**!

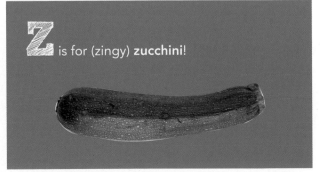

Breakfast Bonanza

The best type of healthy breakfast features a variety of foods from different food groups, such as whole grains; fresh fruit and veggies; and low-fat dairy products, such as milk or yogurt. (You can also use dairy substitutes such as soy milk or almond milk that have been fortified with the same vitamins and minerals provided by dairy foods.)

Eating a balanced breakfast gives children the energy they need to start the day and get through to their next meal or snack. Studies have found that eating a healthy breakfast improves both mood and thinking skills, especially memory, improving children's ability to learn.

In this chapter, you'll find basic recipes for favorite breakfast foods and suggestions for go-withs to round out every meal. Some, such as Rosita's Fresh Pineapple-Mango Smoothie, are quick and easy to make. Others, such as Cookie Monster's Sausage and Zucchini Strata or Abby Cadabby's Very Cherry Multigrain Muffins, can be prepared the night before. Still others, such as Telly's French Toast Triangles, might work best on weekends or any morning when the family can spend a little more time in the kitchen. So . . . happy breakfast, and then, on with the day!

4 CUPS — 32 oz
3 1/2 — 28
CUPS — 24 — 2 2/3
— 20 — 2 1/3
CUPS — 16 — 2
1 1/2 — 12 — 1 1/3
8 — 1
— 2/3

VARIATION
• Substitute cantaloupe, honeydew, or any other type of melon for the watermelon.

Ingredients

2 containers (6 ounces each) low-fat lemon yogurt

8 strawberries

4 ice cream–size scoops watermelon (from half a melon)

1 banana, sliced

1 cup blueberries

1 cup muesli or granola cereal or whole-grain cereal of your choice

Equipment

Measuring cups

Ice cream scoop

Cutting knife

Cutting board

Blender

This looks like an ice cream sundae, but it is really a complete and healthy breakfast in one dish.

1. Combine the yogurt and 4 of the strawberries in a blender. Cover and whirl until smooth. Divide half the mixture among four breakfast bowls or parfait glasses.

2. (kids!) Place a scoop of watermelon in each bowl. Surround with banana slices and blueberries.

3. (kids!) With the help of an adult, pour the remaining yogurt sauce evenly over the fruit.

4. (kids!) Sprinkle each sundae evenly with cereal. Top each with one of the remaining strawberries.

TIP: Watermelon is sweet to eat. It's also full of water—the most important nutrient of all!

This **sundae** will get your Sunday—and your Monday, Tuesday, Wednesday, Thursday, Friday, or Saturday—off to a nice and sunny start!

Ingredients

2 cups fresh pineapple chunks

1 mango, cut up

1½ cups orange juice

1 cup low-fat strawberry or vanilla yogurt (or nondairy yogurt)

Pinch of ground cinnamon

4 fresh strawberries (optional)

Equipment

Measuring cups

Cutting knife

Cutting board

Blender

Serve a smoothie for breakfast along with whole-grain toast triangles and a healthy topping such as Telly's Tomato–White Bean Dippity Dip (page 110).

1. Combine the pineapple, mango, and juice in a blender. (Make sure to keep your children's fingers away from the sharp blender blades.) Whirl on high speed until very smooth, about 1 minute.

 2. kids! Add the yogurt and cinnamon to the blender.

3. Whirl on high speed for 20 seconds longer.

4. kids! Fill four tall drinking glasses with ice cubes.

5. Pour the smoothie over the ice, garnish each glass with a strawberry (if using), and serve.

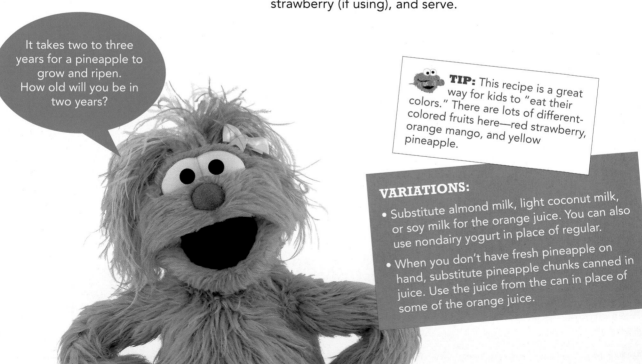

It takes two to three years for a pineapple to grow and ripen. How old will you be in two years?

TIP: This recipe is a great way for kids to "eat their colors." There are lots of different-colored fruits here—red strawberry, orange mango, and yellow pineapple.

VARIATIONS:

- Substitute almond milk, light coconut milk, or soy milk for the orange juice. You can also use nondairy yogurt in place of regular.

- When you don't have fresh pineapple on hand, substitute pineapple chunks canned in juice. Use the juice from the can in place of some of the orange juice.

BEST BUDDIES
Banana Pancakes

Ingredients

1¼ cups all-purpose flour

½ cup wheat germ

1 tablespoon baking powder

½ teaspoon baking soda

½ teaspoon salt

¼ teaspoon ground nutmeg

2 eggs

2 cups (16 ounces) low-fat lemon yogurt

2 bananas, peeled and thinly sliced

Chopped mixed fruit, for topping

Additional lemon yogurt, for topping (optional)

Equipment

Measuring cups

Measuring spoons

Cutting knife

Cutting board

Whisk

Medium bowl

Large bowl

Nonstick griddle or large nonstick skillet

Wide spatula for nonstick pans

Serve pancakes topped with chopped fresh fruit or drippy-ripe berries.

 1. Whisk together the flour, wheat germ, baking powder, baking soda, salt, and nutmeg in a medium bowl.

 2. Crack the eggs into a large bowl. (If any pieces of eggshell fall into the bowl, take them out with your fingers. Wash your hands after you've picked out all the pieces of shell.) Add the yogurt and whisk together the eggs and yogurt until blended.

 3. Stir the flour mixture into the egg mixture until blended.

4. Lightly grease a nonstick griddle or large nonstick skillet over medium heat. Use a ¼-cup measure to pour the batter into the skillet, pouring pancakes several inches apart. Arrange 3 or 4 banana slices over the top of each. Cook on one side until small bubbles appear on the top and the pancake starts to puff, about 1½ minutes. With a wide spatula, carefully turn the pancakes. Cook until the underside is lightly browned, about 1 minute. Repeat with the remaining batter and bananas.

 5. Serve the pancakes topped with mixed fruit and extra yogurt, if you like.

TIP: Bananas have potassium, which is good for your muscles. Bananas are also good for your heart, and they even may make you feel happier. Go bananas for bananas!

VARIATIONS:
- Substitute oat bran or wheat bran for the wheat germ.
- Substitute strawberry, coconut, or tropical fruit–flavored yogurt for the lemon yogurt.
- Substitute blueberries or thinly sliced peaches for the bananas.

21

TELLY'S French Toast Triangles

Ingredients

2 cups strawberries, stems removed

1 cup part-skim ricotta cheese

8 square slices whole-grain bread

3 eggs

⅓ cup low-fat or nonfat milk

½ teaspoon vanilla extract

¼ teaspoon ground cinnamon

1 tablespoon vegetable oil

Unsweetened shredded coconut (optional)

Equipment

Measuring cups

Measuring spoons

Plastic knife

Cutting board

Medium bowl

Fork

Pie plate

Large nonstick skillet

Wide spatula for nonstick pans

Serrated knife

VARIATIONS:

- For a nondairy breakfast, use a mashed banana or two in place of the ricotta cheese.
- In place of the strawberries, use chopped kiwi, raspberries, diced pineapple or mango, or chunky applesauce.

Serve these stuffed sandwich-style French toasts with a glass of milk or orange juice. You can assemble the toasts the night before and store them, covered, in the fridge. The next morning, take them out and let them sit at room temperature for 20 minutes before cooking and serving.

1 *kids!* With supervision, young children can use a plastic knife to cut the strawberries in half. Put half of the strawberries aside, then cut the rest of the strawberries into tiny pieces.

2 *kids!* Combine the ricotta cheese and the tiny pieces of strawberries in a medium bowl. With a fork, stir until well mixed.

3 *kids!* Spread the strawberry mixture evenly on 4 slices of the bread. Top with remaining slices of bread, pressing together gently.

4 *kids!* With a fork, stir together the eggs, milk, vanilla, and cinnamon in a pie plate until well mixed.

5. Heat the oil in a large nonstick skillet over medium heat.

6. In two batches, carefully place each French toast sandwich into the egg mixture; turn to coat the other side. Transfer to the skillet. Cook until golden brown on the underside, about 2 minutes. With a wide spatula, turn and cook until the other side is golden brown, about 2 minutes longer.

7. Transfer the French toast to a cutting board. With a serrated knife, cut each sandwich in half on the diagonal for large triangles. Cut each in half again for smaller triangles.

8 *kids!* Sprinkle the triangles lightly with shredded coconut (if using), and top with the reserved strawberry halves.

TIP: On weekends, or whenever possible, have breakfast together as a family. Eating healthy meals together leads to healthy attitudes about food and eating.

Two large toasted **triangles** or four small toasted **triangles** can be put together to make a square. Try it! Aren't **triangles** terrific?

Does your waffle have a design or pattern? Elmo's waffle has lots of little squares!

Ingredients

1 cup all-purpose flour

⅓ cup whole wheat or multigrain flour

⅓ cup very finely ground almonds or walnuts (or additional flour, if you prefer not to use nuts)

1 teaspoon baking powder

½ teaspoon baking soda

¼ teaspoon salt

2 eggs

1 cup low-fat or nonfat milk

1 cup low-fat plain yogurt

3 tablespoons olive or vegetable oil

2 cups shredded reduced-fat extra-sharp Cheddar or Jarlsberg cheese

Sliced tomato or bell pepper strips, for filling (optional)

Equipment

Measuring cups

Measuring spoons

Cutting knife

Cutting board

Cheese grater

Waffle iron

Medium bowl

Whisk

Large bowl

Ladle

Serve this savory waffle with sliced tomatoes or sweet bell pepper strips. Waffles freeze well, so you can make them in advance and serve these sandwiches even on a busy morning. Just pop the frozen waffles in a toaster to reheat. Look for ground nuts at the store, or grind them yourself with a food processor.

1. Preheat a waffle iron.

2. *kids!* In a medium bowl, whisk together the all-purpose flour, whole wheat flour, ground nuts, baking powder, baking soda, and salt.

3. *kids!* In a large bowl, whisk together the eggs. Add the milk, yogurt, and oil. Whisk until smooth and blended. Whisk in the flour mixture, a little at a time, just until blended. (It's okay if the batter is a little lumpy!)

4. Ladle the batter onto the hot iron, being careful not to overfill. Bake as directed until the waffles are crisp and golden brown, about 5 minutes per batch. Transfer the finished waffles to a plate or cutting board. Repeat with the remaining batter.

5. *kids!* Carefully sprinkle the waffles with the cheese. Top with tomato slices or pepper strips (if using).

6. Serve the waffles open-face, or sandwich 2 waffles together and cut in half before serving.

VARIATION:

• For a sweeter waffle, substitute vanilla yogurt or fruit-flavored yogurt for the plain, and add ½ to 1 teaspoon ground cinnamon. Top with juicy fresh fruit.

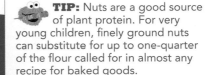

TIP: Nuts are a good source of plant protein. For very young children, finely ground nuts can substitute for up to one-quarter of the flour called for in almost any recipe for baked goods.

25

BIG BIRD'S Easy Cheesy Sure-to-Pleasey Scrambled Eggs on Toast

Ingredients

1 tablespoon olive oil

1 onion, finely chopped

1 cup spinach, finely chopped

¼ teaspoon salt

⅛ teaspoon ground black pepper

6 eggs

½ cup shredded Cheddar cheese

4 slices whole-grain bread

½ cup part-skim ricotta cheese

Equipment

Measuring cups

Measuring spoons

Cutting knife

Cutting board

Cheese grater

Medium nonstick skillet

Spatula for nonstick pans

Medium bowl

Wooden spoon

Toaster or toaster oven

Serve with fresh fruit or a small glass of 100 percent fruit juice.

1. Heat the oil in a medium nonstick skillet over medium heat. Add the onions and cook for 5 minutes. Add the spinach, salt, and pepper. Cook for 1 minute longer.

2. kids! Break the eggs into a medium bowl. Gently stir the eggs with a wooden spoon to break them up slightly.

3. Push the spinach and onion mixture to the side of the skillet. Reduce the heat to low. Add the eggs. Cook, stirring often, for 3 minutes or until almost cooked through, gradually incorporating the spinach mixture. Stir in the Cheddar cheese. Cook for 30 seconds longer.

4. Meanwhile, toast the bread.

5. kids! Spread each slice of toast evenly with ricotta cheese. Place on four serving plates.

6. Top the toast with the scrambled egg mixture and serve.

VARIATIONS:

• Sprinkle the finished eggs with finely chopped fresh basil or other herbs.

• Substitute ½ cup chopped bell peppers or seeded tomatoes for the spinach, and cook them with the onions.

• Substitute soft goat cheese for the ricotta.

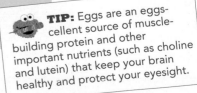 **TIP:** Eggs are an eggs-cellent source of muscle-building protein and other important nutrients (such as choline and lutein) that keep your brain healthy and protect your eyesight.

The biggest bird in the world is the ostrich—some are even bigger than I am! The ostrich also lays the largest eggs. Each egg is about 20 times bigger than the ones you're using in this recipe!

VARIATIONS:
- Substitute soft goat cheese for the ricotta.
- Add 1 tablespoon fresh dill or thyme, or ½ teaspoon dried crumbled dill or thyme, to the egg mixture.

ZOE'S Cutesy Quiche-y Muffins

PREPARATION TIME: 20 MINUTES • BAKING TIME: 20 MINUTES • MAKES 4 SERVINGS (8 MUFFINS)

Ingredients

1 tablespoon olive oil

1 onion, finely chopped

½ cup finely chopped red bell pepper

2 cups baby kale

6 eggs

½ cup part-skim ricotta cheese

⅓ cup grated Parmesan cheese

¼ teaspoon salt

⅛ teaspoon ground black pepper

Equipment

Measuring cups

Measuring spoons

Cutting knife

Cutting board

Cheese grater

8 cup muffin pan

Medium skillet

Medium bowl

Fork

Wooden spoon

Cake tester/toothpick)

Cooling rack

These mini quiches cook quickly and look fun to eat when made in muffin pans. Serve with fresh fruit salad and whole-grain toast.

1. Preheat the oven to 350°F. Lightly oil an 8-cup muffin pan.

2. Heat the oil in a medium skillet over medium heat. Add the onion and cook for 3 minutes. Add the pepper and cook for 5 minutes longer. Stir in the kale and cook for 1 minute, just until wilted.

3. **kids!** In a medium bowl, stir the eggs with a fork until blended. Stir in the ricotta cheese, Parmesan cheese, salt, and pepper.

4. Stir the kale mixture into the egg mixture until blended.

5. **kids!** Use a ⅓-cup measure to divide the mixture evenly among the muffin pan cups.

6. Bake for 15 to 20 minutes, until a cake tester or toothpick inserted in the center of a muffin comes out clean. Transfer the pan to a rack to cool for 1 to 2 minutes. Loosen the muffins from the pan and serve warm.

Quiche is a popular French dish. **Ooh la la!** Find France on a map or globe.

29

ABBY CADABBY'S
Very Cherry Multigrain Muffins

PREPARATION TIME: 15 MINUTES • BAKING TIME: 15 MINUTES • MAKES 12 MUFFINS

Ingredients

1 cup old-fashioned or quick-cooking oats

¼ cup cornmeal

1 cup vanilla or plain low-fat yogurt

1 egg

½ cup olive or vegetable oil

½ cup firmly packed light brown sugar

½ cup all-purpose flour

½ cup whole wheat flour

1 teaspoon baking powder

½ teaspoon baking soda

½ teaspoon salt

¾ cup finely chopped dried cherries

Equipment

Measuring cups

Measuring spoons

Cutting knife

Cutting board

Large bowl

Rubber spatula

12-cup muffin pan and paper cupcake liners or silicone liners and baking sheet

Medium bowl

Whisk

Cake tester/toothpick

Cooling rack

These are great if you need to pack breakfast to go or a snack for later. Serve these muffins with orange, apple, or banana slices and a glass of milk.

 1. In a large bowl, with a rubber spatula, stir together the oats, cornmeal, yogurt, egg, oil, and brown sugar until well mixed. Let stand for 15 minutes while the oven preheats and you prepare the rest of the ingredients.

2. Preheat the oven to 400°F. Lightly oil 12 muffin pan cups, or line with paper cupcake liners. If you are using individual silicone liners, place them on a baking sheet.

 3. In a medium bowl, whisk together the all-purpose and whole wheat flours, baking powder, baking soda, and salt until well mixed. Add to the oat mixture, stirring with the spatula until just combined. Be careful not to overmix. Fold in the cherries. Divide the batter evenly among the prepared muffin cups, using about ⅓ cup per muffin.

4. Bake the muffins for 15 minutes, or until golden on top and a cake tester or toothpick inserted in the center comes out clean. Transfer to a rack to cool for 5 minutes. Turn the muffins out onto a rack to cool further.

VARIATIONS:
- Substitute finely chopped dried cranberries, plums, apricots, raisins, or mixed dried fruit for the cherries.
- Substitute fresh fruit, such as blueberries, finely chopped strawberries, peaches, or pears, for the dried cherries.

Lots of things come in dozens—in groups of 12—just like these muffins. There are **12** eggs in a carton, and there are **12** months in a year. See if you can name them all!

Many layers of strata mean many layers of deliciousness! Here is tricky tongue twister to try. Say five times fast: **six sizzling sausages**. Is your tongue twisted?

COOKIE MONSTER'S
Sausage and Zucchini Strata

PREPARATION TIME: 20 MINUTES • STANDING TIME: 4 HOURS OR OVERNIGHT • BAKING TIME: 45 MINUTES • MAKES 6 SERVINGS

Ingredients

1 teaspoon olive or vegetable oil

8 ounces turkey sausage, casings removed

6 slices whole-grain bread

1 small zucchini, shredded (about 1 cup)

2 cups shredded reduced-fat Jarlsberg or Cheddar cheese

6 eggs

1 tablespoon Dijon mustard

2 cups low-fat milk

Equipment

Measuring cups

Measuring spoons

Box grater

Cheese grater

11 x 7-inch baking dish

Large nonstick skillet

Spatula for nonstick pans

Large bowl

Fork

Wooden spoon

Cake tester (toothpick)

Cooling rack

With bread, eggs, sausage, zucchini, and cheese in one simple layered dish, Cookie's make-ahead strata is a meal all by itself. But it's even better served with fresh fruit or sliced tomatoes.

1. *kids!* Lightly oil an 11 x 7-inch baking dish.

2. Heat the oil in a large nonstick skillet over medium heat. Add the sausage and cook, stirring often, until the meat is cooked through, about 5 minutes.

3. *kids!* Line the baking dish with overlapping slices of bread. Sprinkle the zucchini evenly over the bread.

4. Spoon the sausage over the zucchini.

5. Sprinkle evenly with the cheese.

6. *kids!* In a large bowl, stir the eggs with a fork until broken up. Add the mustard, then the milk, and stir until well blended. Pour the liquid mixture over the bread mixture in the baking dish. Cover and refrigerate for at least 4 hours or overnight.

7. To bake, preheat the oven to 350°F. Uncover the strata and bake until the top is puffy and browned and a cake tester or toothpick inserted in the center comes out clean, about 45 minutes. Transfer the baking dish to a rack to cool for 15 minutes before cutting and serving.

VARIATIONS:

• Substitute ½ cup grated carrot or chopped roasted bell pepper for the zucchini.

• Substitute lean ham or Canadian bacon for the turkey sausage.

• Add 1 tablespoon chopped fresh dill or 1 teaspoon dried to the egg mixture.

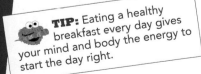

TIP: Eating a healthy breakfast every day gives your mind and body the energy to start the day right.

Ingredients

1 pound small Yukon gold or new red potatoes, cut into ½-inch pieces

1 onion, halved, each half cut into ½-inch pieces

1 red or green bell pepper, halved, seeded, each half cut into ½-inch pieces

1 tablespoon fresh rosemary, chopped, or 1 teaspoon dried, crumbled

1 teaspoon salt

2 tablespoons olive oil

1½ to 2 cups diced leftover (cooked) chicken, turkey, beef, or pork

¼ teaspoon ground black pepper

½ cup reduced-sodium chicken or beef broth

_____

Equipment

Measuring cups

Measuring spoons

Cutting knife

Cutting board

Large rimmed baking sheet or 13 x 9-inch baking pan

Large bowl

Wooden spoon

Large skillet

Save last night's leftover meat for this morning meal. Most of the cooking time is for oven-roasting the vegetables, so you are free to do other things. Serve with cantaloupe or orange slices on the side.

1. Preheat the oven to 400°F. Lightly grease a large rimmed baking sheet or 13 x 9-inch baking pan.

2. **kids!** In a large bowl, combine the potatoes, onion, bell pepper, rosemary, salt, and olive oil. Toss until well combined.

3. **kids!** Spread the vegetable mixture in a single layer on the baking sheet.

4. Roast until the potatoes and vegetables are tender and slightly browned around the edges, 40 to 45 minutes.

5. In a large skillet, combine the meat, roasted vegetables, and black pepper. Add the broth. Heat to a boil over medium heat. Reduce the heat to low and simmer until the broth evaporates, 5 to 8 minutes. Serve warm.

Next time you go to the market, see how many different kinds and colors of potatoes you can find. Some are sweet (which is yucky, but yummy!). Some are white, orange, and red, and some are even purple!

VARIATIONS:

- Substitute sweet potatoes for white potatoes.
- In place of rosemary, flavor this dish with fresh or dried thyme or sage or a mix of herbs.
- To make hash when you don't have leftover meat, buy 8 ounces of thick-cut, lean roast beef or a rotisserie-roasted chicken from the deli section of your supermarket.

TIP: Start with no- and low-sodium packaged food products—less salt is always a healthier choice. If needed, you can always add a little more salt during cooking.

Lunch and Dinner Dishes

Because lunch and dinner dishes are frequently interchangeable, we put them together in one chapter. In fact, lunch can often be made with (delicious) leftovers from last night's dinner; if you can plan it that way, you can save yourself a lot of time. Many main dishes that are cooked and served warm at home, such as **Bert's Turkey Sausage Loaf** and **Grover's Asian Sticky Rice Balls**, can also be packed for travel and enjoyed cold or at room temperature.

Perhaps the biggest difference between these two meals is that family members often split up and go their own way for lunch—off to school or work or the day's errands. When it's time for dinner, it's more likely that everyone is in one place. Try to eat together as a family as often as possible. Family mealtimes not only foster closeness but also help children develop conversation skills and positive attitudes around food and eating. Research shows that families who regularly dine together have children with higher self-esteem, healthier weight, better performance at school, and better interaction with their peers.

VARIATIONS:

- Add finely chopped, seeded tomato and finely chopped fresh basil to the soup at the end of the cooking time.
- Give the chicken broth an Asian flair with a pinch or two of Chinese five-spice powder and a spoonful of soy sauce (instead of salt).
- Add other vegetables, such as thinly sliced zucchini, cut-up green beans, or peas, at the same time as the noodles. If the vegetables are already cooked, add them with the chicken.

Pretend to be cooked noodle and flop all around room. Flop, flop, flop! Try it—it fantastic fun!

COOKIE MONSTER'S
Hearty Chicken Noodle Soup

PREPARATION TIME: 20 MINUTE • COOKING TIME 1 HOUR 20 MINUTES • MAKES 4 MAIN-DISH SERVINGS

Ingredients

BROTH

2½ pounds split chicken breast (on the bone)

2 celery stalks, cut into chunks

1 carrot, cut into chunks

1 large onion, cut into chunks

2 bay leaves

2 sprigs fresh rosemary or 1 teaspoon dried leaves

8 to 10 cups cold water

SOUP

1 tablespoon olive oil

3 carrots, thinly sliced

2 celery stalks, thinly sliced

2 cloves garlic, finely chopped

6 ounces uncooked egg noodles, broken spaghetti, or pasta shapes

Salt and ground black pepper

2 cups baby spinach or kale leaves or chopped regular leaves

Equipment

Measuring cups and spoons

Cutting knife

Cutting board

Large stockpot

Large bowl

Colander or large strainer

Plastic knife

Wooden spoon

Ladle

This is real chicken soup, with homemade broth that simmers for an hour while you do other things. But if you're in a hurry, you can use canned chicken broth and a precooked chicken instead. Serve the soup with crusty whole-grain bread and a crisp salad.

 1. Prepare the broth: Combine the chicken breasts, celery, carrot, onion, bay leaves, and rosemary in a large stockpot. Pour in the water. Add more water, if necessary, to cover the chicken by 1 inch.

2. Place the pot on the stovetop. Heat to a boil over medium-high heat. Reduce the heat to medium-low and simmer gently for 1 hour. Drain the broth into a large bowl through a colander or large strainer. Set the chicken aside and discard the vegetables. Rinse out the pot and wipe dry.

 3. When the chicken is cool enough to handle, discard the skin and bones. With clean hands, shred the chicken meat into bite-size bits. (With supervision, children can also use a plastic knife to cut up the chicken meat.)

4. Prepare the soup: Heat the oil in the pot over medium heat. Add the carrots, celery, and garlic. Cook, stirring often, for 5 minutes, or until the vegetables soften. Add the chicken broth. Heat to a boil. Add the noodles or pasta, and simmer according to the cooking time on the package. Stir in the chicken. Simmer until the chicken is heated through, about 2 minutes more. Taste the broth, and season with salt and pepper.

 5. Divide the baby spinach or kale among four large soup bowls.

6. Ladle the hot soup over the spinach and serve.

ABBY CADABBY'S
Magical Lentil Soup

Ingredients

1 pound (2¼ cups) lentils

2 tablespoons olive oil

1 large onion, finely chopped

3 large cloves garlic, minced

2-inch piece gingerroot, peeled and minced

2 carrots, finely chopped

4 cups water

1 container (14½ ounces) vegetable or chicken broth

1 lemon, halved lengthwise and each half cut into 4 wedges

Salt and ground black pepper

Equipment

Measuring cups

Measuring spoons

Cutting knife

Cutting board

Colander

Large saucepan with cover

Wooden spoon

Ladle

Fresh gingerroot and lemon juice add magical flavor to a classic soup recipe. You can use any color lentil—brown, red, or green, for example—although some hold their shape better than others during cooking. Serve with Elmo's Tiny Tomato Salad (page 96), toasted pita bread, and pineapple cubes.

 1. Pour the lentils into a colander in the sink. Rinse with cool running water, using your hands to sift through the lentils to make sure they all get washed briefly.

2. In a large saucepan, heat the oil over medium heat. Add the onion, garlic, and ginger. Sauté for 5 minutes, stirring occasionally.

3. Stir in the lentils, carrots, water, and broth. Heat to a boil over medium-high heat. Reduce the heat to medium-low, partially cover, and simmer for 30 to 40 minutes, until the lentils are very tender. You can use a handheld blender or potato masher to puree some of the lentils to thicken the soup, if you like. Ladle into individual bowls.

 4. Place a wedge of lemon near each bowl of soup, and tell the soup eaters to squeeze lemon juice into their soup. They can also add their own salt and pepper to taste.

TIP: Lentils are rich in iron, which means they give you lots of energy to grow and go. On nice days, put that energy to use by going on a family walk after the meal.

VARIATIONS:

- Add cooked rice or potatoes for a heartier soup.
- Near the end of cooking time, stir in 2 to 4 cups baby spinach leaves or a mixture of spinach and kale.
- Add 2 teaspoons curry powder to the onion mixture in Step 2.
- Top each serving with a dollop of low-fat plain yogurt.
- Sprinkle each serving with a tablespoon or two of finely chopped fresh cilantro.

VARIATIONS:

- Substitute canned light coconut milk for the low-fat milk.
- If you would like a richer soup, omit the curry powder and stir in ½ cup shredded Cheddar or provolone cheese or grated Parmesan cheese in Step 4. Season to taste.
- Use 1 cup leftover rice or pasta in place of the potato to thicken the soup.
- Substitute other seasonings for the curry powder, such as dried thyme, rosemary, or marjoram.

 **TIP:** Hold on to those leftover cooked veggies! They're full of good-for-you vitamins and minerals and will make this nutritious, delicious soup a breeze!

Grow a potato plant!
Grouches love dirt—but potatoes grow in dirt *or* water! Stick toothpicks around the middle of a potato, then put it in a two-thirds-full container of water so that the toothpicks rest on the rim. Put it in a sunny place. Change the water when it gets cloudy. Watch your plant grow!

OSCAR'S Cream of Any-Old-Thing Leftover Soup

Ingredients

2 tablespoons olive oil

1 onion, finely chopped

2 cloves garlic, finely chopped

½ teaspoon curry powder

1 medium potato, peeled and diced

2 cups chopped leftover cooked vegetables, such as broccoli, cauliflower, carrots, or mixed vegetables

2 cans (14½ ounces each) or 4 cups fat-free, reduced-sodium chicken or vegetable broth

2 slices whole-grain bread, toasted

½ cup low-fat milk (optional)

Salt and ground black pepper

Equipment

Measuring cups

Measuring spoons

Cutting knife

Cutting board

Toaster

Medium saucepan

Plastic knife

Slotted spoon

Food processor

Ladle

Create a quick, filling lunch or supper with this thick vegetable soup. Serve with lean cold cuts or a grain salad, and sliced fresh fruit on the side.

1. Heat the oil in a medium saucepan over medium heat. Add the onion and sauté for 5 minutes. Add the garlic and curry powder and sauté for 1 minute longer. Add the potato, leftover vegetables, and broth. Simmer for 15 minutes, or until the potato and other vegetables are very soft.

2. *kids!* Meanwhile, with a plastic knife, cut the toast into 1-inch squares to use for croutons.

3. Remove the saucepan from the heat and use a slotted spoon to transfer the vegetables to a food processor with some of the broth. Pulse to puree, leaving some chunks of vegetables, if you prefer, or continue until the mixture is smooth, adding more broth from the pan, if necessary.

4. Stir the vegetable puree back into the remaining broth in the saucepan. Cook over medium-low heat to reheat as needed. Add milk for extra creaminess, if you like. Taste and add salt and pepper, if necessary. Ladle the soup into individual bowls.

5. *kids!* Sprinkle each bowl of soup with some croutons, or put all the croutons in a small bowl and pass them around at the dinner table.

Note: Pureed potato gives this soup some of its creaminess, so if the leftover veggies you are using are potatoes, you don't have to add the extra one called for in this recipe.

Ingredients

8 ounces lean ground turkey breast

3 scallions, finely chopped

½ cup grated Parmesan cheese

½ cup whole-grain bread crumbs or quick-cooking oats

2 tablespoons finely chopped fresh basil or 1 teaspoon dried, crumbled

1 clove garlic, minced

½ teaspoon dried oregano

½ teaspoon salt

⅛ teaspoon ground black pepper

2 containers (14½ ounces each) fat-free, reduced-sodium chicken broth

1 can (14½ ounces) diced tomatoes in juice, or 1 large tomato, seeded and diced

2 tablespoons tomato paste

1 package (14 ounces) fresh or frozen cheese, mushroom, or spinach tortellini

Equipment

Measuring cups

Measuring spoons

Cutting knife

Cutting board

Cheese grater

Wooden spoon

Medium bowl

Small spoon

Large saucepan

Ladle

Everyone loves tiny, delicious meatballs! This meal-in-a-bowl needs nothing more than a green salad and slice of bread on the side to round out your lunch or dinner menu.

1 kids! With a wooden spoon, combine the turkey, scallions, ¼ cup of the cheese, the bread crumbs or oats, basil, garlic, oregano, salt, and pepper in a medium bowl until well mixed.

2 kids! With a small spoon and clean hands, roll the turkey mixture into 1-inch meatballs. (Remember not to put your fingers in your mouth when you are preparing meat dishes and to wash your hands when you are finished making the meatballs!)

3. Bring the chicken broth, tomatoes, and tomato paste to a boil in a large saucepan. Add the meatballs and tortellini. Return to a boil, reduce the heat to low, and let simmer for 8 minutes, or until the tortellini are tender and the meatballs are thoroughly cooked.

4. Ladle soup evenly into individual bowls. Sprinkle with the remaining ¼ cup grated Parmesan.

Tortellini are ring-shaped stuffed pieces of pasta. Another name for them is *ombelico*, which means "belly button"—because they are sort of the same shape. Point to your belly button. Is it an innie or an outie?

VARIATIONS:

- Substitute ground chicken or lean ground beef or pork for the turkey.
- Substitute finely chopped fresh flat-leaf parsley for the basil.
- Add fresh baby spinach or kale leaves to the bowl before ladling in the soup.

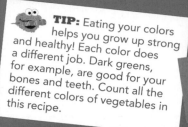

TIP: Eating your colors helps you grow up strong and healthy! Each color does a different job. Dark greens, for example, are good for your bones and teeth. Count all the different colors of vegetables in this recipe.

VARIATION:

• Use a small boiled potato in place of the egg.

BIG BIRD'S Nest Egg Salad

PREPARATION TIME: 10 MINUTES • MAKES 4 SERVINGS

Ingredients

4 hard-cooked (boiled) eggs, shelled

1 avocado, pitted and peeled

4 cups shredded mixed greens for salad

1 carrot, shredded

1 cup fresh, canned, or thawed frozen corn kernels

¼ cup salad dressing of your choice

2 scallions, thinly sliced

Equipment

Measuring cups

Cutting knife

Cutting board

Plastic knife

Box grater

Large bowl

Large spoon

Serve this light yet hearty salad with Cowboy Elmo's Creamy Ranch Dressing (page 103), or any favorite salad dressing, and toast triangles on the side.

 1 Cut each egg in half. Dice the avocado. (Young children can use a plastic knife with adult supervision.) Set aside.

 2 Combine the greens, carrot, corn, and avocado in a large bowl. Add 2 tablespoons of the salad dressing. Toss well to combine.

 3 Arrange the lettuce salad on serving plates to look like nests in the middle of the plate. Top each nest with 2 egg halves, yolk side down. Sprinkle with the scallions. Drizzle the eggs with the remaining 2 tablespoons salad dressing and serve.

Hummingbirds have the smallest nests of all birds, smaller than the size of a walnut. My nest must be one of the biggest, don't you think?

47

ABBY CADABBY'S
Magical Chicken Salad

PREPARATION TIME: 15 MINUTES • MAKES 6 SERVINGS

Ingredients

½ cup low-fat plain Greek-style yogurt

¼ cup reduced-fat mayonnaise

¼ cup orange marmalade or apricot jam

1 teaspoon curry powder

1 teaspoon lime or lemon juice

1 pound cooked chicken breasts, cut into bite-size pieces

2 apples, finely chopped

½ cup finely chopped fresh cilantro

Equipment

Measuring cups

Measuring spoons

Cutting knife

Cutting board

Large bowl

Wooden spoon

Abby thinks this sweet and tangy salad is simply enchanting. Serve this main-dish salad on a bed of shredded crisp romaine lettuce hearts.

1 *kids!* Combine the yogurt, mayonnaise, marmalade or jam, curry powder, and lime or lemon juice in a large bowl. Stir until well blended.

2 *kids!* Add the chicken, apples, and cilantro. Stir until well mixed. Serve at once, or cover and refrigerate to serve later, or pack to go.

Curry is spicy. Marmalade is sweet. What other foods can you think of that are spicy or sweet?

VARIATIONS:
- Substitute turkey or pork for the chicken.
- Substitute finely chopped spinach or fresh flat-leaf parsley for the cilantro.

¡Buen provecho! (Say bwehn proh-VEH-cho.) That's Spanish for "enjoy your meal!"

ROSITA'S Veggie-Cheese Quesadillas

Ingredients

1 tablespoon olive oil

1 cup sliced white mushrooms

8 spinach or tomato-flavored flour tortillas or whole-grain tortillas

2 cups shredded, reduced-fat, extra-sharp Cheddar or Monterey Jack cheese

1 large tomato, seeded and finely chopped

Equipment

Measuring cups

Measuring spoons

Cutting knife

Cutting board

Medium-size skillet

Cheese grater

Wooden spoon

Wide spatula

A quesadilla (pronounced case-a-DEE-yah) is a warm tortilla sandwich that goes great with a small bowl of chili or chicken noodle soup or just a simple salad.

1. Heat the oil in a medium-size skillet over medium heat. Add the mushrooms and cook, stirring often with a wooden spoon, for 3 minutes, or until tender. Set the cooked mushrooms aside to cool, and wipe out the skillet for later use.

2. *(kids)* Lay 4 tortillas on your work surface. Sprinkle the cheese on top, dividing it evenly among the tortillas.

3. *(kids)* Arrange the tomatoes and cooled mushrooms over the cheese. Top with the remaining tortillas.

4. Heat the same skillet over medium heat. Add 1 quesadilla to the skillet. Cook until the bottom is slightly browned and crisp, about 2 minutes. With a wide spatula, carefully turn the quesadilla over, being careful not to spill the filling. Cook until the bottom is crisp and the cheese is melted, 1 to 2 minutes longer. Use the spatula to remove the quesadilla from the skillet. Repeat with the remaining quesadillas.

5. Let each quesadilla cool slightly before cutting into wedges and serving.

VARIATIONS:

- Add very thin slices of lean ham or bits of leftover cooked meat or poultry on top of the vegetables before covering them with the second tortilla.
- Substitute cooked zucchini, peppers, eggplant, greens, or other veggies in place of or in addition to the mushrooms.

TIP: If you want to skip the oil in order to cut back on fat, use a nonstick skillet and cook the mushrooms in a tablespoon or two of water.

GROVER'S Monstrously Delicious Chicken Nuggets Parmesan

PREPARATION TIME: 20 MINUTES • BAKING TIME: 18 MINUTES • MAKES 6 SERVINGS (30 NUGGETS)

Ingredients

1 egg

¼ cup low-fat plain yogurt

1 teaspoon dried oregano

½ teaspoon salt

1¼ cups dried whole-grain bread crumbs

1 pound thin-sliced chicken breasts

1 cup shredded part-skim mozzarella cheese

¼ cup grated Parmesan cheese

2 cups tomato sauce

Equipment

Measuring cups

Measuring spoons

Cutting knife

Cutting board

Cheese grater

Large baking sheet

Medium bowl

Fork

Large plate

Small saucepan

Just like chicken Parmesan but more fun because it's homemade, cut into funky shapes, and saucy! Serve with multigrain spaghetti and steamed broccoli.

1. Preheat the oven to 425°F. Lightly grease a large baking sheet.

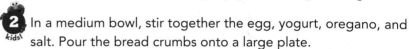 In a medium bowl, stir together the egg, yogurt, oregano, and salt. Pour the bread crumbs onto a large plate.

3. Cut the chicken into 1½- to 2-inch pieces. Add to the bowl with the yogurt mixture and toss to coat.

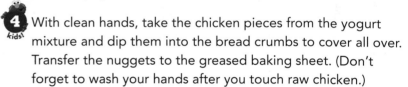 With clean hands, take the chicken pieces from the yogurt mixture and dip them into the bread crumbs to cover all over. Transfer the nuggets to the greased baking sheet. (Don't forget to wash your hands after you touch raw chicken.)

5. Bake the nuggets for 15 minutes, or until cooked through. Carefully remove from the oven and sprinkle evenly with the mozzarella and Parmesan cheeses. Return to the oven for 2 minutes to melt the cheese.

6. Meanwhile, in a small saucepan, heat up the tomato sauce. Spoon the sauce onto serving plates and top with nuggets.

TIP: These nuggets are healthier than their fast-food versions because they are baked instead of fried. Try this same method with crumb-coated fish fillets.

VARIATION:
• Coat the nuggets with finely crushed whole-grain crackers, wheat germ, or very finely ground almonds or hazelnuts instead of the bread crumbs.

Elmo thinks it's fun to smell the foods as you cook. Smell the mustard. Smell the cooked veggies. Smell the finished mac and cheese when it cools down. **Yum!** That makes Elmo hungry!

ELMO'S Mac 'n' Cheese 'n' Bits

PREPARATION TIME: 10 MINUTES • BAKING TIME: 1 HOUR • MAKES 8 SERVINGS

Ingredients

2 cups 4%-fat cottage cheese

8 ounces extra-sharp Cheddar cheese, cut up

2½ cups low-fat milk

2 tablespoons olive oil

2 teaspoons Dijon mustard

½ teaspoon salt

⅛ teaspoon ground black pepper

8 ounces (2 cups) uncooked multigrain or high-fiber elbow pasta or other small pasta shape

1 cup cooked peas or chopped spinach or kale, or 2 cups cooked broccoli or cauliflower in bite-size pieces

½ cup whole-grain bread crumbs (optional)

Equipment

Measuring cups

Measuring spoons

Cutting knife

Cutting board

2½-quart baking dish

Food processor

Large bowl

Wooden spoon

Aluminum foil

Cooling rack

Why is this a great macaroni and cheese recipe when you're in a hurry? Because you can skip the step of cooking the macaroni separately before combining it with cheese and baking! Who knew? (Elmo knew!) Serve this quick-to-fix, veggie-packed baked pasta dish with a side salad or a bowl of tomato soup.

1. Preheat the oven to 375°F. Lightly oil a 2½-quart baking dish.

2. Whirl the cottage cheese in a food processor for 2 minutes, or until very smooth. Add the cheese and whirl for 1 minute. Add the milk, oil, mustard, salt, and pepper. Whirl until blended. (If you are using a blender or small processor, you may have to puree the mixture in two batches.)

3 kids! Pour the uncooked pasta into a large bowl. With a wooden spoon, stir in the peas or other vegetable.

4. Pour the cheese mixture into the bowl with the pasta and veggies.

5 kids! Stir the pasta, veggies, and cheese mixture with the wooden spoon until well mixed.

6. Turn the pasta and cheese mixture into the prepared baking dish. Cover with foil.

7. Bake for 30 minutes. Uncover and stir. Sprinkle with the bread crumbs (if using). Bake, uncovered, for 20 minutes longer. Transfer to a rack and let stand for 10 minutes before serving.

VARIATIONS:
- Add 1 can (14½ ounces) diced tomatoes, drained, with the other vegetables.
- Add ½ cup chopped roasted sweet red peppers with the other vegetables.

 TIP: Pureed cottage cheese adds lots of flavor and creaminess to recipes but less fat than other types of cheese.

GROVER'S Lemony Linguine with Zucchini and Cherry Tomatoes

PREP TIME: 15 MINUTES • COOKING TIME: 15 MINUTES • MAKES 4 SERVINGS

Ingredients

8 ounces uncooked multigrain linguine

1 medium zucchini, halved and thinly sliced

1 pint cherry or grape tomatoes

3 tablespoons olive oil

2 large cloves garlic, finely chopped

1 tablespoon chopped fresh oregano leaves or 1 teaspoon dried, crumbled

½ teaspoon salt

¼ teaspoon ground black pepper

¼ teaspoon crushed red pepper flakes (optional)

1 tablespoon lemon juice

½ cup grated Parmesan cheese

Equipment

Measuring cups

Measuring spoons

Cutting knife

Cutting board

Plastic knife

Large pot

Large skillet

Wooden spoon

Colander

For a light and simple lunch or supper, serve with a sliced multigrain baguette.

1. Heat a large pot of lightly salted water to boiling. Add the linguine and cook according to the package directions. Add the zucchini 3 minutes before the end of cooking time.

 Meanwhile, cut the tomatoes in half. (Small children can use a plastic knife with adult supervision.)

3. In a large skillet, heat the oil over medium heat. Add the tomatoes, garlic, oregano, salt, black pepper, and red pepper flakes (if using). Cook, stirring, for 1 minute. Turn off the heat, stir in the lemon juice, and season, if needed, with additional salt and pepper to taste.

4. Drain the pasta and zucchini in a colander. Add to the tomato mixture in the skillet. Toss gently, reheat if necessary, and serve at once.

 Pass the grated cheese at the table so each person can add some to the pasta.

VARIATIONS:

• Substitute trimmed, sliced green beans or asparagus for the zucchini.

• Substitute chopped sun-dried tomatoes for the cherry tomatoes.

• Substitute basil for the oregano—or use both herbs together.

• Add small cubes of fresh mozzarella cheese.

• Add chopped cooked turkey bacon, lean ham, or chicken.

• Use whichever type of pasta you prefer.

When I traveled to Italy, I noticed that people there eat lots of pasta and tomatoes. Find Italy on a map or globe. It is shaped like an adorable little boot!

ERNIE'S Light and Easy Veggie Lasagna Rolls

PREP TIME: 25 MINUTES • COOKING TIME: 25 MINUTES • MAKES 4 SERVINGS (8 ROLLS)

Ingredients

8 uncooked lasagna noodles

2 cups baby kale or spinach leaves, finely chopped

1 cup low-fat cottage or part-skim ricotta cheese, or a blend of the two

1 cup shredded part-skim mozzarella cheese

½ cup grated Parmesan cheese

¼ cup finely chopped fresh basil or flat-leaf parsley

2 cloves garlic, finely chopped

½ teaspoon salt

⅛ teaspoon ground black pepper

1½ cups tomato sauce

Equipment

Measuring cups

Measuring spoons

Cutting knife

Cutting board

Cheese grater

9-inch square pan

Large pot

Large bowl

Wooden spoon

Small spoon

Lasagna is even more lovable and easy to eat rolled up. Serve with lean, grilled Italian-style turkey sausages and Elmo's Tiny Tomato Salad (page 96) on the side.

1. Preheat the oven to 350°F. Lightly grease a 9-inch square baking pan.

2. Heat a large pot of lightly salted water to boiling. Cook the lasagna noodles until they are *al dente*, or firm-cooked.

3. Meanwhile, in a large bowl, with the wooden spoon, combine the kale or spinach, cottage cheese, ½ cup of the mozzarella cheese, ¼ cup of the Parmesan cheese, the basil, garlic, salt, and pepper.

4. Use a small spoon to spread about ¼ cup of the cheese mixture evenly over the length of each noodle. Roll each noodle up.

5. Place the lasagna rolls, seam side down and side by side, in the greased pan.

6. Spoon the tomato sauce evenly over the rolls. Sprinkle evenly with the remaining ½ cup mozzarella and ¼ cup Parmesan cheeses.

7. Bake for 20 minutes, or until the sauce is bubbly and the rolls are heated through.

VARIATIONS:

• Substitute mixed greens for the kale.

• Add 1 cup leftover shredded chicken or turkey or thinly sliced cooked sausage to the filling.

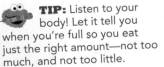

TIP: Listen to your body! Let it tell you when you're full so you eat just the right amount—not too much, and not too little.

OSCAR'S Shrimp Fried Rice Mess

Ingredients

2 tablespoons vegetable oil

8 ounces shelled shrimp, chopped

4 eggs

1 sweet red pepper, finely chopped

1 carrot, finely chopped

1 bunch scallions, thinly sliced

2 cloves garlic, minced

1-inch piece gingerroot, minced

3 cups cold cooked basmati or jasmine rice (from 1 cup uncooked)

½ cup frozen peas

2 tablespoons reduced-sodium soy sauce

2 teaspoons toasted sesame oil

Salt and ground black pepper

¼ cup finely chopped fresh cilantro

Equipment

Measuring cups

Measuring spoons

Cutting knife

Cutting board

Large nonstick skillet

Wooden or nonstick spoon

Large bowls (2)

Medium bowl

Fork

The best fried rice is made with leftover rice, or rice that is cooked in advance and cool when added to the skillet.

1. Heat 1 tablespoon of the vegetable oil in a large nonstick skillet over medium heat. Add the shrimp and cook, stirring often with the wooden spoon, for 3 minutes. Transfer the shrimp to a large bowl and set aside.

2. (kids!) Stir the eggs with a fork in a medium bowl.

3. Add the eggs to the skillet and cook over medium-low heat, stirring often. Chop into small pieces and transfer to the bowl with the shrimp.

4. (kids!) Separate the pepper, carrot, scallions, garlic, and ginger into piles of different colors on a cutting board or plate.

5. (kids!) Stir up the rice in a large bowl to make it easier to cook.

6. Heat the remaining 1 tablespoon vegetable oil in the skillet over medium heat. Sauté the red pepper and carrot for 2 minutes. Add the scallions, garlic, and gingerroot and sauté for 2 minutes, stirring often.

7. Add the rice to the skillet, stirring to mix in the vegetables and break up any clumps. Stir in the peas, soy sauce, and sesame oil. Stir in the reserved shrimp and eggs and cook, stirring often, until well mixed and heated through, about 2 minutes. Stir in salt and pepper to taste. Remove the skillet from the heat and stir in the cilantro.

VARIATIONS:

- Substitute uncured turkey bacon for the shrimp.
- Add a finely chopped tomato or 1 cup cherry tomato halves during the last minute of the cooking time.

 TIP: Take small bites and talk together about the textures and tastes of the dish as you eat—is it crunchy, chewy, salty, spicy? Recipes like this are not only healthy and delicious, but they also help build vocabulary!

VARIATIONS:

- Spice up the mix with a few drops of hot sauce, sweeten with Chinese hoisin (BBQ) sauce, or give the balls a tangy bite by adding 1 tablespoon fresh lemon juice with the soy sauce.

- For a more authentic rice ball, add crushed nori (dried seaweed).

- Use any finely chopped vegetables, such as mushrooms, bell peppers, celery, or radish, in place of the carrot or cucumber.

- Substitute turkey bacon, leftover cooked ground or finely chopped meat, tofu, or another meat alternative for the tuna, salmon, or ham.

I love foods that are shaped in balls. What other cute and adorable round foods can you think of?

Ingredients

1 cup Arborio rice or other short-grain rice

2 cups water

¼ teaspoon salt

1 teaspoon vegetable oil

½ cup finely diced carrot

½ cup finely chopped onion

½ cup finely diced cucumber

1 hard-cooked (boiled) egg

1 can (6 ounces) chunk light tuna or salmon, or ½ cup finely diced uncured ham

2 tablespoons reduced-sodium soy sauce

1 teaspoon toasted sesame oil

½ to 1 cup sesame seeds, toasted (see Note)

Equipment

Measuring cups

Measuring spoons

Cutting knife

Plastic knife

Cutting board

Medium saucepan

Medium nonstick skillet

Medium bowl

Wooden or nonstick spoon

Plastic food-handling gloves or small, thin, plastic food storage bags

Small skillet

These Korean-style rice balls can be served warm for dinner with a stir-fry or other Asian-style dish. They are also good cold, so they can travel with an ice pack in a lunch box to work or school.

1. Combine the rice, water, and salt in a medium saucepan. Heat to a boil over medium heat. Reduce the heat to low, cover, and cook for 17 minutes. Remove the pan from the heat and set aside, covered, until it has slightly cooled and you are ready to make the rice balls.

2. In a medium nonstick skillet, heat the vegetable oil over medium heat. Add the carrot. Sauté, stirring often, for 2 minutes. Add the onion and cucumber. Sauté for 2 minutes longer.

3. (kids!) Cut the hard-cooked eggs into tiny pieces with a plastic knife. Put the pieces in a medium bowl. Stir in the fish or ham. Add the carrot, onion, and cucumber to the bowl.

4. (kids!) Stir the rice into the bowl. Add the soy sauce and sesame oil and stir again until well mixed.

5. (kids!) Place plastic gloves or small plastic food bags over your hands. Scoop out a little bit of the rice mixture and shape it into a small ball. Roll some or all of the balls in the toasted sesame seeds. Place each rice ball on a platter and repeat with the remaining rice.

NOTE: To toast sesame seeds, heat a small skillet over medium heat. Add the seeds and toast, stirring often, until golden brown, 2 to 3 minutes. Immediately transfer the seeds from the skillet to a plate to prevent burning.

ROSITA'S Chicken Taco Burgers with Mexi-Cali Salad

PREPARATION TIME: 20 MINUTES • COOKING TIME: 7 MINUTES • MAKES 4 SERVINGS

Ingredients

BURGERS

1 pound ground chicken

1 onion, finely chopped

½ cup chopped fresh cilantro

⅓ cup uncooked quick-cooking oats

1 teaspoon chili powder

½ teaspoon salt

⅛ teaspoon ground black pepper

SALAD

2 tablespoons olive oil

1 tablespoon lime juice

4 cups mixed baby greens

1 cup cherry tomatoes, halved

½ cucumber, peeled, seeded, sliced

1 avocado, pitted, peeled, diced

1 small red onion, halved and thinly sliced

1 cup shredded Cheddar cheese

Equipment

Measuring cups

Measuring spoons

Cutting knife

Cutting board

Cheese grater

Large bowls (2)

Wooden spoon

Broiler pan

Whisk

Meat thermometer

Serve these taco-flavored burgers on top of the hearty salad, with mango or pineapple cubes on the side or tossed over the salad. For a festive look, decorate the dish with the shredded cheese, which looks almost like confetti.

1. Preheat the broiler with the top rack 4 inches from the heat source. Lightly oil a broiler pan.

 2. Prepare the burgers: Combine the ground chicken, onion, cilantro, oats, chili powder, salt, and pepper in a large bowl. Stir with the wooden spoon to mix well. Use clean hands to shape into 4 small balls, then flatten into 4 burgers. Place on the oiled broiler pan. (Don't forget to wash your hands well again after this step!)

3. Broil the burgers for 3 minutes. Turn and broil for 3 to 4 minutes longer, until thoroughly cooked through (the meat will no longer be pink in the center, and an instant-read thermometer inserted in the center of each burger will register 165°F).

 4. Meanwhile, prepare the salad: Whisk together the olive oil and lime juice in a large bowl. Add the greens, tomatoes, cucumber, avocado, and onion. Toss gently to combine.

 5. Divide the salad among the serving plates.

6. Top each salad with a burger. Sprinkle evenly with cheese and serve.

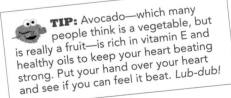
TIP: Avocado—which many people think is a vegetable, but is really a fruit—is rich in vitamin E and healthy oils to keep your heart beating strong. Put your hand over your heart and see if you can feel it beat. *Lub-dub!*

VARIATIONS:

- Substitute ground turkey or lean ground beef for the chicken.
- Substitute chopped romaine lettuce, spinach leaves, or shredded raw cabbage for the mixed baby greens.
- Add bell pepper strips, grated carrot, jicama, or any vegetables you like to the salad.

Some people call avocados "alligator pears": pears because of their shape, and alligators for their green color and tough skin. But avocados don't bite you—*you bite them!*

TIP: Traditional "sloppies" get their sweetness from added sugar; in this recipe, just as much sweetness comes from the grated carrots, concentrated tomato paste, and a touch of balsamic vinegar.

Can you think of a rhyme for **sloppy**? I can—my **sloppy jalopy**! How about a rhyme for **ham**? That's right—**SCRAM!** Yeah, I'm talking to you!

Sloppy OSCARS

Ingredients

1 tablespoon olive oil

1 pound ground chicken or turkey

1 onion, finely chopped

1 celery stalk, thinly sliced

2 carrots, grated

2 cloves garlic, finely chopped

1 can (15 ounces) or 2 cups reduced-sodium tomato sauce

¼ cup tomato paste

1 tablespoon balsamic vinegar

1 teaspoon reduced-sodium soy sauce

½ teaspoon salt

⅛ teaspoon ground black pepper

4 to 6 hearty or soft whole-grain buns

Equipment

Measuring cups

Measuring spoons

Cutting knife

Cutting board

Box grater

Large nonstick skillet

Large bowl

Wooden spoon

Enjoy this version of sloppy joes with side orders of corn or potato salad, coleslaw, and Grover's Homemade Refrigerator Pickles (page 100).

1. Heat 1 teaspoon of the oil in a large nonstick skillet over medium heat. Add the ground meat and cook, stirring often and breaking up clumps, just until all the meat has cooked through, about 5 minutes. Transfer the meat to a large bowl and set aside.

2. Heat the remaining 2 teaspoons oil in the same skillet over medium heat. Add the onion and cook for 3 minutes. Add the celery and cook for 3 minutes longer. Add the carrots and garlic and cook for 1 minute longer.

3. *(kids)* Stir the tomato sauce, tomato paste, vinegar, soy sauce, salt, and pepper into the bowl with the cooked chicken.

4. Stir the chicken mixture back into the skillet. Cover and simmer over low heat for 15 minutes.

5. *(kids)* Open up the buns and place one on each serving plate.

6. Top the buns with the meat sauce and serve.

VARIATIONS:

- Substitute 1 cup finely chopped red bell pepper for the carrots. Substitute 1 cup sliced mushrooms for the celery.
- Serve the "sloppies" over rice, quinoa, pasta, or another grain food instead of the traditional soft buns.
- If you are out of tomato paste, you can substitute an equal amount of ketchup.

BERT'S Turkey Sausage Meat Loaf

Ingredients

1 pound lean ground turkey breast

8 ounces Italian-style turkey sausage, casing removed, if necessary

1 carrot, shredded (about 1 cup)

1 onion, grated or finely chopped (about 1 cup)

⅓ cup oat bran

¼ cup finely chopped fresh flat-leaf parsley

1 egg

½ teaspoon salt

¼ teaspoon ground black pepper

Equipment

Measuring cups

Measuring spoons

Box grater

Cutting knife

Cutting board

Small shallow baking pan

Aluminum foil

Large bowl

Wooden spoon

Meat thermometer

Cooling rack

Serve slices of this tasty loaf with Cookie Monster's Me-Love-Warm-Green-Bean Salad (page 92) and mashed potatoes. Use leftover meat loaf for sandwiches.

1. Preheat the oven to 350°F. Line a small shallow baking pan with aluminum foil. Lightly coat the foil with vegetable oil.

2. kids! In a large bowl, combine the ground turkey, sausage, carrot, onion, oat bran, parsley, egg, salt, and pepper. Use a large wooden spoon to stir until well mixed.

3. kids! With clean hands, help shape the turkey mixture into a loaf and place in the prepared pan. (Remember to wash your hands again after you touch raw meat.)

4. Bake for 50 minutes, or until an instant-read thermometer inserted in the center of the loaf reads 165°F and the meat is no longer pink. Transfer the pan to a rack and let the meat loaf stand for 10 minutes before slicing and serving.

VARIATIONS:

• Substitute an equal amount of finely chopped mushrooms, sweet peppers, or other vegetables for the carrot.

• Substitute an equal amount of whole-grain bread crumbs, uncooked quick-cooking or instant oats, or cooked rice, barley, or quinoa for the oat bran.

TIP: When you use ground turkey breast and lean turkey sausage for your recipes in place of traditional ground meat and sausage mixtures, you cut the fat content in half. Adding veggies and oatmeal adds vitamins and fiber and improves the texture of the loaf.

Parsley and pepper begin with the letter "P." So do pots and pans. What other "P" words can you find in the kitchen?

October 4 is National Taco Day. Find it on your calendar. But you can eat tacos any day you like!

Ingredients

2 tablespoons lime juice

1 tablespoon olive oil

¾ teaspoon salt

1 pound mild fish fillets, such as tilapia, turbot, cod, or pollock, or your family's favorite fish

½ cup low-fat plain Greek-style yogurt

¼ cup finely chopped fresh cilantro

⅛ teaspoon ground black pepper

3 cups finely shredded green cabbage

1 small tomato, seeded and finely chopped

½ cup finely chopped yellow, red, or orange bell pepper

1 avocado, pitted and peeled

8 (6-inch) flour or corn tortillas

Fresh cilantro sprigs, for serving

Equipment

Measuring cups

Measuring spoons

Cutting knife

Cutting board

Box grater

Spoon

Medium bowls (2)

Fork

Plastic knife

Broiler pan

Serve these soft tacos with sweet corn and sliced ripe mango, or with Rosita's Special Salsa (page 99).

 1 Stir together 1 tablespoon of the lime juice, the olive oil, and ¼ teaspoon of the salt in a medium bowl. Add the fish and stir gently to coat the fillets with the oil mixture. Set aside. (Wash your hands before you continue if you touched raw fish.)

 2 Combine the yogurt, cilantro, remaining 1 tablespoon lime juice, remaining ½ teaspoon salt, and the black pepper in another medium bowl. Stir with a fork until well mixed. Stir in the cabbage, tomato, and sweet pepper. Set aside.

 3 With adult supervision, small children can use a plastic knife to cut the avocado into small cubes. Set aside.

4. Preheat the broiler. Arrange an oven rack so that it is 4 inches from the heat source.

5. Place the fish fillets on a broiler pan. Broil until the fish flakes easily with a fork and is opaque in the center, 4 to 6 minutes, turning once halfway through cooking, if possible. Transfer the fillets to a cutting board and break up into large chunks.

6. Meanwhile, place the tortillas on serving plates or in a basket for all at the table to serve themselves.

 7 Show everyone how to pile some fish, cabbage slaw, and avocado into the middle of a tortilla. Top with sprigs of cilantro. Fold the tortilla over to eat.

VARIATIONS:
- Substitute shrimp for the tilapia.
- Substitute shredded crisp lettuce, such as romaine hearts, for the cabbage.

TIP: Fish is good for your muscles and your heart. It also may have a strong taste—make a point of trying different kinds of fish to see which your family prefers.

GROVER'S Gado-Gado

Ingredients

1 teaspoon vegetable oil

1 small onion, very finely chopped (½ cup)

2 or 3 cloves garlic, very finely chopped

¾ cup peanut butter, almond butter, or other nut butter

2 tablespoons reduced-sodium soy sauce

2 tablespoons lemon juice

2 cups water

¼ to ½ teaspoon hot sauce, or to taste (optional)

4 cups assorted raw and/or cooked vegetables (such as raw bean sprouts, shredded cabbage, shredded or sliced carrots, steamed green beans, potato cubes, broccoli and cauliflower, cut into bite-size pieces, if necessary)

12 ounces cooked boneless chunks chicken or turkey

6 hard-cooked (boiled) eggs, halved or quartered

½ cup finely chopped fresh cilantro (optional)

Equipment

Measuring cups

Measuring spoons

Cutting knife

Cutting board

Box grater

Medium saucepan

Small bowl

Grover's all-time favorite dish from Indonesia is nothing more than a good selection of raw and cooked veggies with poultry or meat, served with a lightly seasoned nut butter dipping (or dripping!) sauce. Gado-gado literally means "mix-mix."

1. Heat the oil in a medium saucepan over medium-low heat. Add the onion and sauté for 5 minutes. Add the garlic and sauté for 1 minute longer.

 Stir together the nut butter, soy sauce, and lemon juice in a small bowl.

3. Add the peanut butter mixture to the saucepan. Stir in the water until well mixed. Heat to a boil over medium heat; reduce the heat to low and simmer until the sauce thickens, 15 to 20 minutes. Add the hot sauce if you like your sauce a little spicy.

 Arrange the vegetables, meat, and eggs on a platter or individual plates, separating foods by their color. Sprinkle everything with the cilantro (if using). Pour the sauce into individual ramekins and serve.

NOTE: You can make the sauce up to 5 days in advance. Refrigerate and gently reheat before serving. Taste and, if necessary, adjust the seasonings at that point.

VARIATION:
- Add steamed shrimp to the mix.

TIP: Be adventurous! Try new foods and flavors from all around the world! Taste foods from your own family's cultures and traditions.

The country of Indonesia is very very far away. It is made up of more than 13,000 little islands. Whew! That would take a long time to count, even for Count von Count! How high can *you* count?

VARIATIONS:

- Substitute chunks of turkey, pork tenderloin, or lean beef for the chicken.
- For a vegetarian version, omit the meat and add tofu, more beans, or vegetarian meat substitutes.
- Omit the smoked paprika and increase the chili powder to 1 tablespoon.
- Substitute 2 ounces dark chocolate, chopped, for the cocoa powder.

Chocolate is a secret ingredient in chili—it makes the chili taste even better. Did you know that chocolate comes from little brown beans called cacao beans?

Chilly Outside? ELMO'S Chili Inside!

Ingredients

2 sweet potatoes, cut into ½-inch cubes

2 sweet red or green peppers, cut into ½-inch squares

¼ cup olive oil

1 large onion, finely chopped

4 cloves garlic, finely chopped

1 tablespoon smoked sweet paprika

1 teaspoon chili powder

1 teaspoon salt

1 pound boneless chicken, cut into 1-inch chunks

2 tablespoons unsweetened cocoa powder

2 cans (15½ ounces each) black beans, rinsed and drained

2 cans (14½ ounces each) diced tomatoes with green chiles (mild) or diced tomatoes with Jalapeño peppers (spicy)

2 cups water or low-sodium chicken or vegetable broth

½ cup finely chopped fresh cilantro

Equipment

Measuring cups

Measuring spoons

Cutting knife

Cutting board

Rimmed nonstick baking sheet

Large bowl

Wooden spoon

Large stockpot

This sweet and smoky flavored chili is perfect for a cold day. To stretch the number of servings, ladle it over hot cooked rice. Serve with a crisp green salad topped with avocado cubes or a bowl of Rosita's Special Salsa (page 99). If you like, serve with optional toppings like low-fat yogurt, shredded reduced-fat cheese, or avocado cubes.

1. Preheat the oven to 375°F. Lightly oil a rimmed nonstick baking sheet.

2. Combine the sweet potatoes and peppers in a large bowl. Add 1 tablespoon of the oil and toss with the wooden spoon to coat. Spread the vegetables in a single layer on the oiled baking sheet.

3. Roast the vegetables for 25 minutes, or until tender.

4. Meanwhile, heat the remaining 3 tablespoons oil in a large stockpot over medium heat. Add the onion and sauté for 5 minutes. Stir in the garlic, paprika, chili powder, and salt; sauté for 1 minute longer.

5. Add the chicken to the stockpot. Sauté, stirring often, for 5 minutes. Stir in the cocoa powder. Add the beans, tomatoes, and water or broth. Reduce the heat to low and simmer gently, stirring occasionally, until the meat is tender, 30 to 45 minutes.

6. Stir the roasted sweet potatoes and peppers into the chili. Simmer for 15 minutes longer.

7. Sprinkle each bowl of chili with chopped cilantro and serve.

Pizza Party on Sesame Street!

PREPARATION TIME: 30 MINUTES • RISING TIME: 1 HOUR 15 MINUTES • BAKING TIME: 18 MINUTES •
MAKES 8 SERVINGS (TWO 12-INCH PIES OR 8 INDIVIDUAL PIES)

Ingredients

DOUGH

1 cup lukewarm water (95°–105°F)

1 teaspoon sugar

1 envelope (2½ teaspoons) active dry yeast

2 cups all-purpose flour

1 cup whole wheat flour

1 teaspoon salt

2 tablespoons olive oil

Cornmeal, for dusting baking sheet

TOPPINGS

2 cups tomato sauce

3 cups colorful selection of cooked chopped vegetables, such as steamed broccoli, roasted sweet peppers, sautéed white mushrooms, and artichoke hearts

2 cups shredded part-skim mozzarella cheese

1 cup grated Parmesan cheese

Equipment

Measuring cups

Measuring spoons

Cheese grater

1-cup glass measuring cup

Food processor or large bowl

Wooden spoon

Large baking sheets or 12-inch pizza pans (2)

Large bowl

Cooling racks

A choose-your-own-topping theme encourages everyone to get involved. If you're having a bigger party, just double the recipe!

1. Prepare the dough: In a 1-cup glass measuring cup, combine the water and sugar. Sprinkle the yeast over the mixture and let stand for 5 minutes, or until frothy. Stir and let stand for 5 minutes longer.

2. In a food processor or large bowl, combine the all-purpose flour, whole wheat flour, and salt. Whirl or stir until mixed. Stir the oil into the yeast mixture.

3. In the food processor, with the motor running, add the liquid mixture through the feed tube and process until the dough comes together in a slightly sticky mass. Or in the bowl, make a well in the flour mixture, add the liquid mixture, and stir until a soft dough forms. Turn the dough out onto a floured work surface.

4 kids! With the help of a grown-up, with clean hands, knead the dough until smooth and elastic, 5 to 10 minutes. Divide the dough into 2 flattened rounds of equal size. Let the dough rest for at least 10 minutes or up to 1 hour. (You can refrigerate or freeze the dough at this point, if you wish. Flatten the dough and wrap each round in plastic wrap or freezer-proof wrap. If frozen, allow the dough to thaw in the refrigerator before proceeding with the recipe.)

5 kids! Place the dough in a clean, greased bowl and turn the dough to grease all over. Cover with a kitchen towel and let the dough rise for 45 minutes. Punch the dough down, cover with a kitchen towel, and let rise for 30 minutes longer.

(Continued on page 78)

TIP: Use any mixture of cheeses you like—combine reduced-fat and regular cheeses to cut back on the fat. Challenge your child to make the pizza as veggie-colorful as possible.

VARIATIONS:

• For a white pizza, skip the tomato sauce and cover the pie with a thin layer of ricotta cheese, then continue with the recipe as directed.

• Add toppings such as sliced fresh tomatoes, olives, or scallions, or chopped fresh herbs such as basil or rosemary.

6. Preheat the oven to 450°F.

7. Lightly sprinkle cornmeal on 2 baking sheets or round pizza pans. With the help of a grown-up, press or roll each round of dough out to a 12-inch circle. Or, divide each round into 4 equal pieces of dough and press or roll each into an individual 6-inch circle.

8. Prebake larger crusts for 8 to 10 minutes and smaller crusts for 6 to 8 minutes, until lightly browned. Transfer to a work surface to cool slightly.

9. Divide the sauce evenly over the pizzas. Layer your choice of vegetables over the sauce. Sprinkle with the mozzarella and Parmesan cheeses.

10. Bake for 8 to 10 minutes, until the toppings are heated through and the edge of the crust is crisp and browned. Transfer to racks and let stand for 5 minutes before serving.

How would you divide a pizza pie for two hungry monsters so that each gets a fair share? How about for four hungry monsters? Eight? Draw a round pizza on a piece of paper and see!

PIZZA PARTY!

Share some jokes and fun facts at your pizza party!

FUN FACT
Americans eat about 350 slices of pizza per second.

JOKE
How do you fix a broken pizza? With tomato paste!

JOKE
What does an aardvark like on its pizza? Ant-chovies!

FUN FACT
Pepperoni is the most popular topping.

JOKE
What is a dog's favorite pizza? PUP-eroni!

JOKE
What do you call a sleeping pizza? piZZZZzzza!

JOKE
Why did the man open a pizza shop? He wanted to make some dough!

How many pepperoni slices can you count on this pizza pie?

Side Dishes and Staples

Side dishes help round out a meal and offer an extra way to provide nutrients in children's diets. Vegetables and fruits featured in sides bring a naturally wide variety of colors, textures, and shapes to the plate to help make meals more appealing and engaging, whether simply, as in **Bert's Maple Butternut Stripes**, or more creatively, as in **Rosita's Double Corn Cakes with Rosita's Special Salsa**. When children help prepare these dishes and watch the foods go from whole to chopped to cooked, they develop a better appreciation for the dishes served at the table. It may take a few tries before children like a new food; be patient and keep trying. Introducing fun and interesting words to describe the color, smell, texture, and taste of foods—words such as smooth, squishy, crunchy, creamy, bitter, or sweet— may encourage them to give new ones another chance.

Homemade staples are foods you can keep on hand for at least a day or two, or even up to a week, to use for multiple meals or snacks. As with other types of homemade food, when you make **Cookie Monster's Homemade Nut Butter** or **Grover's Homemade Refrigerator Pickles**, you have the opportunity to show your children how to prepare popular foods in more wholesome ways. By making these at home, you control the salt, sugar, and fat that go into these foods, which can help children develop a taste for healthier foods. You may find that your homemade version simply tastes better!

There are more than 100 different kinds of **quinoa**! Can you count to 100? Now try counting to 100 by tens! Ah, ah, ah, wonderful!

COUNT von COUNT'S
Cranberry-Apple Quinoa

PREPARATION TIME: 15 MINUTES • COOKING TIME: 15 MINUTES • MAKES 4 SERVINGS

Ingredients

1 cup quinoa, well rinsed

2 cups water

2 apples

2 celery stalks

2 scallions

¾ cup dried cranberries

1 cup baby spinach or kale leaves

¼ cup orange juice

3 tablespoons olive oil

Salt and ground black pepper

Equipment

Measuring cups

Measuring spoons

Cutting knife

Cutting board

Medium saucepan

Fork

Large bowl

Whisk

Wooden spoon

Serve this warm and fruity quinoa as a side dish with meat, poultry, or fish, or as a vegetarian main dish for lunch or dinner. You can also serve leftovers cold the next day as a salad, though you may need to moisten it with a little more olive oil and lemon juice.

1 kids! Put the quinoa in a medium saucepan. Pour in the water.

2. Bring to a boil over medium heat. Reduce the heat to medium-low and simmer until the quinoa is tender and the water is absorbed, 10 to 15 minutes. Fluff gently with a fork.

3. Very finely chop the apples, celery, scallions, dried cranberries, and spinach or kale.

4 kids! Whisk together the orange juice and olive oil in a large bowl. With a wooden spoon, stir in the apples, celery, scallions, cranberries, and spinach or kale.

5. Stir in the cooked quinoa and toss to mix well. Add salt and pepper to taste.

NOTE: For very small children, it may be necessary to steam or sauté the apples, celery, scallions, dried cranberries, and spinach or kale to soften before adding to the quinoa.

VARIATIONS:

• Substitute balsamic vinegar for the lemon juice, or use a mixture of both.

• Substitute chopped dried cherries, raisins, or mixed chopped dried fruit for the cranberries.

• Add other chopped fresh fruit, such as mango, melon, peaches, grapes, or oranges.

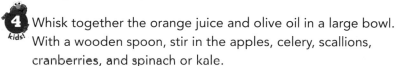 **TIP:** Quinoa (pronounced *KEEN-wah*) is one of the healthiest foods of all. It's high in protein and iron, and it's gluten-free. Quinoa is actually not a grain at all—it's a relative of spinach, chard, and beets. The part we eat is the seed!

BIG BIRD'S Sunny Sweet Potatoes

PREPARATION TIME: 10 MINUTES • BAKING TIME: 55 MINUTES • MAKES 4 SERVINGS

Ingredients

4 medium sweet potatoes

½ cup part-skim ricotta cheese

1 cup chunky applesauce, plain or flavored with other fruit (you can use Bert and Ernie's Peary Delicious Applesauce on page 114)

Equipment

Measuring cups

Vegetable scrubber

Fork

Cutting knife

Cutting board

Wooden spoon

Fork

Spoon

These fruity, baked sweet potatoes go well with turkey, chicken, ham, or any type of meat, and they are also a delicious addition to any meal with a Southwestern, Mexican, or Indian theme.

1. To bake the potatoes in a conventional oven, preheat the oven to 400°F.

2. Help a grown-up scrub the potatoes so they are very clean.

3. Pierce the potatoes all over with a fork and place in an oven-safe or microwave-safe pan. Bake until tender, about 45 minutes in a conventional oven or 20 to 25 minutes on High power on a carousel in a microwave oven.

4. Slice the baked potatoes lengthwise, about halfway down, and push at both ends to open. (The potatoes will be hot, so you may want to handle with potholders.) Use a fork to mash the potatoes in their skins. Mash 2 tablespoons of cheese into each potato.

5. Just before serving, spoon the applesauce evenly on top of the potatoes.

VARIATIONS:
- Omit the cheese and simply top the potatoes with applesauce.
- To make a main dish out of baked sweet potatoes, top with the meat sauce from Sloppy Oscars (page 67) or Chilly Outside? Elmo's Chili Inside! (page 75), or a similar saucy topping.

TIP: Sweet potatoes are a superfood. They pack a lot of good nutrition into a small package, especially if you eat the skin, too. Beta-carotene, which gives them their bright orange color, also helps keep your eyes healthy!

I thought **sweet potatoes** were always orange. But sometimes sweet potatoes are red, or even purple. Wow! I didn't know that. Which color do you like best?

VARIATION:

• Substitute lemon juice, red or white wine vinegar, or any flavored vinegar for the balsamic vinegar.

OSCAR and SLIMEY'S
Roasted Root Veggies

PREPARATION TIME: 10 MINUTES • ROASTING TIME: 55 MINUTES • MAKES 6 TO 8 SERVINGS

Ingredients

¼ cup olive or vegetable oil

¼ cup balsamic vinegar

2 tablespoons honey

2 tablespoons fresh rosemary leaves, chopped, or 2 teaspoons dried, crumbled

1 teaspoon salt

4 beets, peeled and cut into 1-inch chunks

2 turnips, peeled and cut into 1 inch chunks

1 large sweet potato, peeled, halved, and cut into 1-inch chunks

1 large onion, peeled, halved, and each half cut into quarters

8 ounces thick baby carrots, halved, or regular carrots, cut into 1-inch chunks

6 to 8 cloves garlic, halved, or quartered if very large

¼ teaspoon ground black pepper

Equipment

Measuring cups

Measuring spoons

Cutting knife

Cutting board

13 x 9-inch baking pan

Whisk

Large spoon

Serve these hearty veggies with roast meat or poultry and a grainy side dish, such as Count von Count's Cranberry-Apple Quinoa (page 83), or a simple rice dish.

1. Preheat the oven to 375°F.

 In a 13 x 9-inch baking pan, whisk together the oil, vinegar, honey, rosemary, and salt.

 Add the beets, turnips, sweet potato, onion, carrots, and garlic to the pan. Stir gently to coat all of the vegetables with the honey mixture.

4. Roast for 50 minutes, or until all the vegetables are tender and browned, stirring several times during cooking. Sprinkle with pepper and serve.

Root vegetables grow under the ground. That's Slimey's neighborhood! Say *roasted roots* five times fast!

ABBY CADABBY'S
Magical Squish-Squash

PREPARATION TIME: 10 MINUTES • COOKING TIME: 7 MINUTES • MAKES 4 SERVINGS

Ingredients

2 medium yellow summer squash or golden zucchini

1 tablespoon olive oil

½ cup grated Parmesan cheese

Equipment

Measuring cups

Measuring spoons

Plastic knife

Cheese grater

Kitchen towel

Medium nonstick skillet

Wooden spoon

Serve this cheesy, grated zucchini dish with any meal, even with eggs for breakfast!

1 kids! With adult supervision, use a plastic knife to trim the stem end from each squash.

2 kids! Place a clean kitchen towel on your work surface.

3. Use a cheese grater to shred the squash over the center of the towel.

4 kids! Fold the edges of the towel over the squash and press lightly to absorb some of the liquid from the squash.

5. In a medium nonstick skillet, heat the oil over medium heat. Add the zucchini and cook, stirring often with a wooden spoon, until very tender, 5 to 8 minutes. Stir in the cheese and serve.

Summer squash has vitamins A, B, and C, just like the first three letters of the alphabet! Twinkle think: What other foods can you think of that begin with A, B, or C?

VARIATIONS:

- Use green zucchini instead of yellow, or a combination of both.
- Add finely chopped fresh flat-leaf parsley or dill, or a combination, while cooking the squash.

TIP: Yellow and orange foods, like the summer squash in this recipe, help boost your immune system—which means they may help you stay healthy.

VARIATIONS:

• Substitute sweet potatoes or other types of winter squash for the butternut squash.

• For a spicy treat, replace the cinnamon and maple syrup with curry powder or Chinese five-spice powder, then toss with the oil.

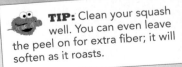 **TIP:** Clean your squash well. You can even leave the peel on for extra fiber; it will soften as it roasts.

BERT'S Maple Butternut Stripes

PREPARATION TIME: 20 MINUTES • ROASTING TIME: 35 MINUTES • MAKES 6 TO 8 SERVINGS

Ingredients

1 small butternut squash

1 teaspoon ground cinnamon

½ teaspoon salt

2 tablespoons maple syrup

2 tablespoons olive oil

Equipment

Measuring spoons

Large rimmed baking sheet

Aluminum foil

Cutting knife

Cutting board

Large bowl

Wooden spoon

Serve this cinnamon-sweet winter squash side dish with Sloppy Oscars (page 67), or with any meat, poultry, or grain dish (like Count von Count's Cranberry-Apple Quinoa on page 83). Use leftovers to make Oscar's Cream of Any-Old-Thing Leftover Soup (page 43).

1. Preheat the oven to 400°F. Line a large baking sheet with rimmed sides with aluminum foil. Lightly oil the foil.

2. Cut the squash into 2 x ¼ x ¼-inch sticks, or "stripes." (Some sticks will have to be shorter than 2 inches because of the shape of the squash, but try to keep them all ¼ inch wide and thick for even cooking.)

3. *kids!* In a large bowl, stir the squash stripes and cinnamon with a wooden spoon until well mixed. Sprinkle with the salt. Add the maple syrup and olive oil. Toss to coat well.

4. *kids!* Place the stripes in rows on the greased baking sheet. Pour any syrup-oil mixture left at the bottom of the bowl over the stripes.

5. Roast until tender, 30 to 35 minutes.

> What other things can you find at home that have **stripes**? Which stripes are vertical (up and down), like the ones on my shirt? Which are horizontal (side to side), like the ones on the shirt Ernie wears?

Ingredients

1 pound green beans

2 tablespoons olive oil

2 tablespoons balsamic vinegar

2 cloves garlic, finely chopped

¼ teaspoon salt

⅛ teaspoon ground black pepper

2 plum tomatoes, finely chopped

Equipment

Measuring spoons

Cutting knife

Cutting board

Colander

Steamer tray (for pot)

Pot

Large bowl

Whisk

Large spoon

Serve as a warm side dish with meat, poultry, or fish, or refrigerate to serve cold or send with a boxed lunch.

1 *kids!* Put the beans in a colander and rinse. Snap the stem end off each green bean. Throw the stem ends away. Snap each bean in half.

2. Place the steamer tray in a medium pot. Add water to reach just beneath the tray. Put the green beans in the tray. Bring the water to a simmer over low heat and steam for 4 to 6 minutes, or until tender-crisp.

3 *kids!* Meanwhile, whisk together the olive oil, vinegar, garlic, salt, and pepper in a large bowl. Add the tomatoes to the bowl.

4. Drain the green beans in a colander. Add to the bowl with the tomatoes and dressing.

5 *kids!* Toss the beans, tomatoes, and dressing with a large spoon until well mixed. Serve warm or at room temperature.

Green beans sometimes called "string beans" or "snap beans." When you finish snapping beans for recipe, go snap-happy and snap your fingers, too!

VARIATIONS:

- Add ¼ cup finely chopped fresh flat-leaf parsley or basil.

- Add feta cheese, goat cheese, or cubes of provolone cheese for a heartier salad.

- Substitute 1 cup finely chopped roasted red pepper for the tomatoes.

TIP: Don't be discouraged if kids don't like a new food the first time they try it. It can take many tries before—ta-da!—success.

VARIATIONS:

• Add a tablespoon or two of finely chopped fresh cilantro to the batter.

• Add ½ teaspoon chili powder to the batter.

• Top the pancakes with plain yogurt instead of, or in addition to, the salsa.

TIP: Shop for food with your kids and make an adventure of it. When possible, buy fresh vegetables and fruits that are in season.

ROSITA'S Double Corn Cakes

PREPARATION TIME: 15 MINUTES • COOKING TIME: 20 MINUTES • MAKES 6 SERVINGS (36 SMALL PANCAKES)

Ingredients

½ cup all-purpose flour

¼ cup fine cornmeal

½ teaspoon baking powder

½ teaspoon salt

6 ounces (¾ cup) low-fat plain yogurt

2 eggs

1 cup well-drained corn kernels

1 tablespoon vegetable oil

Rosita's Special Salsa (page 99) or other salsa

½ avocado, finely chopped (optional)

Equipment

Measuring cups

Measuring spoons

Cutting knife

Cutting board

Small bowl

Whisk

Medium bowl

Large nonstick skillet

Pancake spatula for nonstick pan

Spoon

Serve these savory little pancakes as a side dish with meat, poultry, or fish, topped with Rosita's Special Salsa (page 99) and with sliced avocado.

1 Combine the flour, cornmeal, baking powder, and salt in a small bowl. Whisk together until well blended.

2 Combine the yogurt and eggs in a medium bowl. Whisk together until well blended. Whisk in the flour mixture, just until blended. Gently stir in the corn.

3. In a large nonstick skillet, heat the oil over medium heat. Add batter, 1 tablespoon at a time, for each pancake. Reduce the heat to medium-low and cook for 1 to 2 minutes, until bubbles form on the top of the pancakes. Flip the pancakes over and cook for 1 minute longer, or until the underside is lightly browned. Repeat until all the batter is used. (You can pile the pancakes on a large plate and keep them warm in a 200°F oven until ready to serve.)

4 Spoon a little bit of salsa and some avocado (if using) over the pancakes before serving.

How many corn cakes in the picture have a tiny triangle avocado slice on top? How many corn cakes are plain? How many corn cakes are there all together?

95

ELMO'S Tiny Tomato Salad

Ingredients

1 tablespoon olive oil

1 tablespoon balsamic vinegar

½ teaspoon salt

⅛ teaspoon ground black pepper

1 pint cherry tomatoes

1 cup pimiento-stuffed green olives

1 small red onion, finely chopped

Equipment

Measuring cups

Measuring spoons

Cutting knife

Cutting board

Medium salad bowl

Whisk

Plastic knife

Spoon

Cherry tomatoes are always tasty, and they are available year-round. This salad goes with anything, even with the scrambled eggs you have for breakfast!

 1 *kids!* In a medium salad bowl, whisk together the olive oil, vinegar, salt, and pepper.

 2 *kids!* With a plastic knife, cut each tomato in half. Cut the olives in half. Add the tomatoes and olives to the bowl with the dressing. Stir in the onion. Use a spoon to toss gently to mix.

When something is cut in half, that means there are two equal pieces. Next time you have a cookie or a piece of fruit, **give half to a friend!** Elmo thinks you are a very good sharer!

96

VARIATIONS:

• Add 2 teaspoons finely chopped fresh rosemary leaves or 1 teaspoon dried, crumbled.

• Substitute pitted ripe olives for the green olives.

TIP: Red fruits and vegetables, like the tomatoes in this recipe, are good for your heart.

VARIATIONS:
- Substitute diced cucumber for the bell pepper.
- Substitute peach, plum, apple, or pear for the mango or other fruit that may be out of season.

⬤ ROSITA'S Special Salsa

PREPARATION TIME: 20 MINUTES • MAKES 2 CUPS

Ingredients

1 large mango, finely chopped

1 small red, yellow, or orange bell pepper, finely chopped

1 cup finely chopped watermelon

1 cup finely chopped fresh pineapple

¼ cup finely chopped red onion (optional)

1 jalapeño pepper, seeded and very finely chopped

2 tablespoons lime juice

2 tablespoons balsamic vinegar

¼ cup finely chopped fresh cilantro (optional)

Equipment

Measuring cups

Measuring spoons

Cutting knife

Plastic knife

Cutting board

Medium bowl

Large spoon

Serve this tropical fruit salsa with seafood, chicken, burgers, or any Mexican-style dish (like Rosita's Soft Fish Tacos with Slaw on page 71). For a snack, serve with whole-grain tortilla chips. Feel free to double, triple, or even quadruple the recipe to feed a crowd.

 1 kids! Combine the mango, bell pepper, watermelon, pineapple, onion (if using), and jalapeño pepper in a medium bowl. Add the lime juice and vinegar. Stir together with a large spoon.

 2 kids! Cover and refrigerate the salsa until ready to serve. Just before serving, add the cilantro (if using) and gently stir. Store leftovers in the refrigerator for up to 2 days.

NOTE: If preparing more than several hours ahead, add the lime juice, vinegar, and cilantro just before serving.

The word *salsa* is Spanish for "sauce" or "relish." It's also the name of a dance. Make up your own special dance while you snack on **salsa!**

GROVER'S Homemade Refrigerator Pickles

PREPARATION TIME: 15 MINUTES • COOKING TIME: 2 MINUTES • MAKES 6 PICKLES

Ingredients

6 mini seedless cucumbers or
1 large seedless cucumber

4 sprigs fresh dill

1 cup water

1 cup cider vinegar

1 bay leaf

6 cloves garlic, crushed

2 teaspoons sea salt or kosher salt

½ teaspoon whole black peppercorns

_____

Equipment

Measuring cups

Measuring spoons

Cutting knife

Plastic knife

Cutting board

Small saucepan

Quart-size jar or bowl with lid

Funnel

Pickles go with everything! Insert an ice pop stick into one end of a pickle for a "pickle on a stick" snack.

1 kids! Wash the cucumber(s) and rinse the dill. If using the large cucumber, slice it with a plastic knife or have the adult slice the cucumber.

2 kids! With adult supervision, pack the cucumbers and dill into a clean, quart-size jar or glass bowl.

3. In a small saucepan, combine the water, vinegar, bay leaf, garlic, salt, and peppercorns. Heat to a boil over medium heat. Reduce the heat to low and simmer for 1 minute.

4. Carefully pour the vinegar mixture through a funnel over the cucumbers. Cover and let stand until completely cool.

5. Put the covered pickle jar or bowl into the refrigerator and leave it there for at least 8 hours or up to 5 days before serving.

Hey, Zoe! Why was the cucumber mad?

Because it was in a pickle!

VARIATIONS:

- Many different raw vegetables can be pickled the same way: Try trimmed carrot sticks, green beans, cauliflower florets, okra, or bell pepper strips.
- Substitute sprigs of fresh herbs such as rosemary, thyme, tarragon, or oregano for the dill, or use a mixture.

TIP: Homemade pickles contain much less salt than the store-bought kind. Talk with your kids about where the cucumbers in this pickle recipe grow, and where other vegetables grow as well, before they get to the supermarket.

VARIATION:
• Add ½ cup crumbled feta, goat, or blue cheese.

COWBOY ELMO'S
Creamy Ranch Dressing

PREPARATION TIME: 10 MINUTES • MAKES 2 CUPS (8 TO 12 SERVINGS)

Ingredients

1½ cups low-fat plain yogurt

¼ cup low-fat mayonnaise

¼ cup grated onion

2 cloves garlic, finely chopped

1 tablespoon lemon juice

1 teaspoon chopped fresh dill or ¼ teaspoon dried

1 teaspoon salt

⅛ teaspoon ground black pepper

¼ cup chopped fresh flat-leaf parsley

Equipment

Measuring cups

Box grater

Measuring spoons

Cutting knife

Cutting board

Large bowl

Whisk

Spoon

Make this tasty dressing with regular yogurt to use as a salad dressing or with thicker Greek yogurt to use as dip for raw and steamed veggies.

1 kids! Combine the yogurt, mayonnaise, onion, garlic, lemon juice, dill, salt, and pepper in a large bowl. Whisk until blended.

2 kids! Stir in the parsley.

3. Store the dressing in the refrigerator for up to 5 days.

Look for different colors and shapes of tomatoes at the market to dip in your ranch dressing. What colors and shapes can you find? Yippee-aye-oh, partner!

COOKIE MONSTER'S
Homemade Nut Butter

PREPARATION TIME: 5 MINUTES • MAKES 1¾ CUPS

Ingredients

1 pound (about 3 cups) unsalted or lightly salted shelled nuts, such as dry-roasted peanuts, almonds, or cashews

1 to 1½ tablespoons olive or vegetable oil

¼ teaspoon salt (optional)

Water (optional)

Equipment

Measuring cups

Measuring spoons

Large bowl

Large spoon

Food processor

Rubber spatula

2-cup storage container with lid

Cookie Monster loves peanut butter, but he also loves almond butter, cashew butter, and even sunflower seed butter! He uses all these butters the same way: for a simple snack of nut butter spread on toast or sliced apple, for nut butter and banana sandwiches, and in one of Grover's favorite recipes called Gado-Gado (page 72), which has a dee-licious sauce made with nut butter!

1 **kids!** In a large bowl, combine the nuts and 1 tablespoon of the oil. With a large spoon, stir to mix well.

2. Pour the oiled nuts into a food processor and add the salt (if using). Process until very smooth, 2 to 3 minutes. Add an additional ½ tablespoon oil toward the end of processing, if necessary. For thinner nut butter, add water, 1 tablespoon at a time, and process until it reaches the desired consistency.

3. With a rubber spatula, transfer the nut butter back to the large bowl.

4 **kids!** Spoon the nut butter into a 2-cup storage container with a tight-fitting lid. Store in the refrigerator for up to 2 weeks, and stir before serving.

Peanuts look like nuts, but surprise! Not nuts at all. They legumes. They grow underground. Above ground they have pretty little blossoms. Me nuts about peanuts!

VARIATIONS:

- Use sunflower seeds, mixed nuts, or a mixture of seeds and nuts.
- Use a nut or seed oil, such as peanut, sunflower, or walnut oil, in place of the olive or vegetable oil. The oil doesn't have to match the nut.

TIP: This recipe shows children that the nut butters purchased in the market are actually made from a whole food. It also gives you control of the type of oil you use, as well as the sugar and salt content. Nut butters are packed with protein, which makes them ideal to use at breakfast or lunch when you need lots of energy!

Snacks and Desserts

Between-meal snacks are important for children, who use up energy at a much higher rate than adults do and need to replenish their fuel more often. Look at snacks as "mini meals" and incorporate the same balance of wholesome ingredients you would for breakfast, lunch, or dinner. Keep a batch of **Telly's Tomato–White Bean Dippity Dip** in the fridge to serve with cut-up veggies. Snack on **Big Bird's Seed Crackers**, spread with **Cookie Monster's Homemade Nut Butter**, and enjoy a small bowl of **Bert and Ernie's Peary Delicious Applesauce** on the side.

For sweet treats at the end of everyday dinners, fruit is always a colorful, healthy, and tasty option. For family celebrations and special occasions such as birthdays and holidays, baking homemade cookies and cakes together can create sweet memories. When you try **Zoe's Sweet and Special Birthday Cake** or **Cookie Monster's Favorite Molasses Crackle Cookies**, you'll see that it's easy to cut back on sugar and saturated fats and to incorporate ingredients that add nutrients, fiber, and healthy oils—all without losing the wow factor and great taste of a luscious dessert.

VARIATIONS:

- Substitute whole wheat, oat, or mixed-grain flour for half of the all-purpose flour. To make oat flour, whirl ½ cup quick-cooking oats in a blender or food processor for 30 seconds, or until it turns into flour.

- Add 2 tablespoons dried rosemary leaves to the blender with the larger seeds.

Before you break the baked dough into little crackers, count how many squares there are in each row across. Then count how many are in each row down. How many crackers will that make all together? Go crackers for crackers!

BIG BIRD'S
Homemade Seed Crackers

PREPARATION TIME: 20 MINUTES • BAKING TIME: 25 MINUTES • MAKES 4 DOZEN CRACKERS

Ingredients

1 cup shelled, dry-roasted pumpkin seeds, sunflower seeds, or a combination of both

1 cup all-purpose flour

1 teaspoon onion powder or garlic powder (optional)

½ teaspoon salt

⅓ cup water

¼ cup olive or vegetable oil

¼ cup sesame seeds

Equipment

Measuring cups

Measuring spoons

Food processor or blender

Medium bowl

Wooden spoon

Baking sheet

Rolling pin

Table knife or pizza wheel

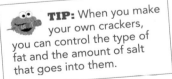

TIP: When you make your own crackers, you can control the type of fat and the amount of salt that goes into them.

Top these hearty crackers with peanut butter or Cookie Monster's Homemade Nut Butter (page 104) and a banana slice, thin slices of cheese with sliced apple on the side, or hummus. Or serve them as part of a veggie and cracker platter with Cowboy Elmo's Creamy Ranch Dressing (page 103) and Telly's Tomato–White Bean Dippity Dip (page 110).

1. Preheat the oven to 350°F. Whirl the seeds in a food processor or blender until finely chopped. (For children under age 4, be sure there are no whole seeds larger than a sesame seed.)

2. In a medium bowl, stir together the flour, onion or garlic powder (if using), and salt with a wooden spoon. Stir in the water, oil, chopped seeds, and sesame seeds until well mixed.

3. Place the dough in the center of a baking sheet. With a lightly floured rolling pin, gently spread the dough out into a 16 x 12-inch rectangle of even thickness.

4. With a table knife or pizza wheel, score the dough into forty-eight 1½-inch squares (8 crosswise scores and 6 lengthwise scores).

5. Bake in the preheated oven for 10 minutes. Carefully turn the baking sheet one half turn and bake for 10 minutes longer. Turn off the oven and leave the crackers in the oven, with the door closed, until crisp, about 1 hour.

6. When cool enough to handle, break the crackers along the scored lines. Store the crackers in a covered container for up to 2 weeks.

TELLY'S
Tomato–White Bean Dippity Dip

PREPARATION TIME: 10 MINUTES • COOKING TIME: 10 MINUTES • MAKES 3 CUPS (9 TO 12 SERVINGS)

Ingredients

2 tablespoons olive oil

1 onion, finely chopped

4 cloves garlic, finely chopped

2 teaspoons sweet smoked paprika

½ teaspoon ground cumin

2 cans (19 ounces each) cannellini (white kidney) beans, with liquid

Salt and ground black pepper

1 tomato, seeded and very finely chopped

½ cup green or ripe olives, pitted and chopped

_____

Equipment

Measuring cups

Measuring spoons

Cutting knife

Cutting board

Medium skillet

Wooden spoon

Food processor or blender

Slotted spoon

Medium bowl

Smoked paprika gives this creamy dip a bacon-like smokiness without adding any bacon. Serve with raw veggie dippers such as bell pepper slices, celery or jicama sticks, and cucumber rounds, or with whole-grain crackers or triangles of toast.

1. Heat the oil in a medium skillet over medium heat. Add the onion and sauté until tender, about 5 minutes. Add the garlic, paprika, and cumin and sauté for 1 minute longer. Stir in the beans and their liquid with a wooden spoon. Cook until warmed through, about 2 minutes.

2. With a slotted spoon, transfer the bean mixture to a food processor or blender, using about ¼ cup of the liquid. Whirl until very smooth, about 2 minutes, adding a spoonful more bean liquid at a time to achieve a dipping and spreading consistency. Transfer to a medium bowl and add salt and pepper to taste.

3 Stir the tomato and olives into the bean dip.

4 kids! Serve the bean dip or put it in a covered container and store in the refrigerator for up to 2 days.

VARIATIONS:
- Use black beans, pink beans, or other beans in place of the cannellini beans.
- Add a small jar of drained, chopped roasted red peppers to the dip in place of, or in addition to, the chopped tomatoes.
- Add ½ cup finely chopped fresh cilantro or flat-leaf parsley before serving.

TIP: Beans are one of the best vegetable sources of protein, iron, fiber, and other important nutrients. Bravo for beans!

I wonder how many words you can think of that rhyme with **bean**. Here's a hint for one rhyming word: It's the color of Oscar's fur.

OSCAR'S Green-Like-Me Smoothie

PREPARATION TIME: 10 MINUTES • MAKES 4 SERVINGS

Ingredients

2 cups kale, spinach, or a mixture

1 avocado, pitted, peeled, and cut up

1 banana

1-inch piece gingerroot, peeled and halved (optional)

1 cup apple juice

½ cup cold water

Equipment

Measuring cups

Cutting knife

Cutting board

Blender

Rubber spatula

A wonderfully nutritious snack on its own, this delicious, sweet-tasting smoothie would also go well with a turkey sandwich or a piece of meat or chicken, in place of a fruit or veggie side dish.

 1. Use your hands to tear the kale, spinach, or other greens into smaller pieces.

2. Combine the greens, avocado, banana, and gingerroot (if using) in a blender. (Make sure to keep your children's fingers away from the sharp blender blades.) Whirl on high speed until smooth, about 1 minute.

 3. Pour the apple juice and water into the blender.

4. Cover the blender and puree until very smooth, scraping down the side of the container with a rubber spatula and adding more water, if necessary, for a thinner consistency.

5. Fill tall drinking glasses with ice and add a straw if you like.

6. Pour the smoothie over the ice.

VARIATIONS:

- Use peaches, mango, or almost any type of soft, ripe fruit in place of, or in addition to, the banana. (Encourage your child to notice how different fruits and juices change the color of the drink.)
- Substitute cranberry juice, grape juice, or other juice for the apple juice, or just use more water instead of juice to cut back on sweetness.

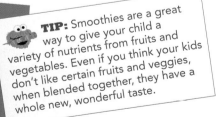

TIP: Smoothies are a great way to give your child a variety of nutrients from fruits and vegetables. Even if you think your kids don't like certain fruits and veggies, when blended together, they have a whole new, wonderful taste.

Ingredients

6 apples, mixed varieties, peeled, cored, and cut into 1-inch chunks

2 cups water

2 tablespoons lemon juice

4 Anjou or Bartlett pears, peeled and cored

2 tablespoons light brown sugar (optional)

1 teaspoon ground cinnamon

½ teaspoon ground nutmeg

½ teaspoon vanilla extract

Equipment

Measuring cups

Measuring spoons

Vegetable peeler

Cutting knife

Cutting board

Large saucepan

Wooden spoon

Plastic knife

Large bowl

Potato masher

For a snack, serve this chunky pear applesauce with a dollop of low-fat yogurt. At dinnertime, pair it with roast meat, poultry, or fish. At lunchtime, you can serve a dish of applesauce with anything!

1. Combine the apples, water, and lemon juice in a large saucepan. Bring to a boil over medium-high heat. Reduce the heat to medium-low and simmer, stirring occasionally with a wooden spoon, until the apples begin to soften, about 10 minutes.

 2. Use a plastic knife to cut the pears into small pieces.

3. Stir the pears, brown sugar (if using), cinnamon, and nutmeg into the saucepan. Simmer, stirring occasionally, for 10 minutes. Transfer the applesauce to a large bowl. Stir in the vanilla. Set aside until the applesauce cools down. Taste and then adjust sugar and seasonings, if necessary.

 4. Use a potato masher to smash the apples and pears into a chunky sauce. Cover the bowl and put the applesauce in the refrigerator so you can serve it cold.

VARIATIONS:
- To make peach applesauce, substitute 5 peaches for the pears.
- To make strawberry applesauce, omit the pears and add 2 cups halved strawberries in Step 3.

VARIATIONS:
• Substitute pieces of other ripe fruit, such as peaches, nectarines, or plums, for up to half of the berries.
• Serve with lemon yogurt, lemon pudding, or a half-half combination of whipped cream and yogurt.

ZOE'S No-Bake, Make-Ahead Berry Delicious Summer Pudding

PREPARATION TIME: 20 MINUTES • REFRIGERATOR TIME: 24 HOURS • MAKES 6 SERVINGS

Ingredients

4 cups mixed raspberries, blackberries, and cut-up strawberries (about 1¾ pounds total)

3 tablespoons sugar

3 tablespoons water

6 to 8 slices bread (depending on the size of the slices): oat bran bread, oatmeal bread, or whole-grain bread

Low-fat vanilla yogurt or vanilla pudding, for serving

Equipment

Measuring cups

Measuring spoons

Cutting knife

Cutting board

Medium saucepan

Plastic knife or cookie cutter

Quart-size bowl

Large spoon

Saucer or small plate

Thin spatula

Serve this super-easy, fruity, molded bread pudding with a dollop or drizzle of yogurt or vanilla pudding.

1. In a medium saucepan, combine the berries, sugar, and water. Heat just to boiling over medium-high heat. Reduce the heat to medium-low and simmer, gently stirring once or twice, for 2 minutes. Remove the pan from the heat and set aside until cool enough to handle.

2. Meanwhile, cut the crusts from the bread. Set 1 slice aside. With a plastic knife or cookie cutter, cut 1 slice into a circle large enough to fit in the bottom of a 1-quart bowl. Place the bread circle in the bowl.

3. Cut the remaining bread into 1-inch-wide rectangles. Fit the rectangles around the side of the bowl to cover the inside of the bowl completely.

4. Use a spoon to transfer the fruit to the bowl, covering up the bread.

5. Place the set-aside piece of bread over the fruit in the bowl to make a "lid." If it doesn't cover the fruit, use extra bread rectangles to fill in the space. Place a saucer or small plate on top of the bread lid. Place something heavy, like a can of beans or broth, on the saucer to weigh it down.

6. Refrigerate for 24 hours. To serve, remove the weight and the saucer. Run a thin spatula or knife around the edge of the pudding to loosen the bread from the bowl. Invert a large plate or small platter over the bowl, then invert the plate and bowl together to unmold the pudding. Serve with vanilla yogurt or pudding.

117

COOKIE MONSTER'S
Favorite Molasses Crackle Cookies

PREPARATION TIME: 20 MINUTES • BAKING TIME: 30 MINUTES • MAKES 4 DOZEN COOKIES

Ingredients

1 cup all-purpose flour

1 cup whole wheat flour

⅓ cup oat bran

1½ teaspoons baking soda

1 teaspoon ground cinnamon

½ teaspoon ground cloves

½ teaspoon ground ginger

½ teaspoon salt

⅔ cup sugar

½ cup plus 2 tablespoons vegetable oil

⅓ cup molasses

1 egg

Additional sugar, for rolling

Equipment

Measuring cups

Measuring spoons

Whisk

Medium bowl

Large bowl

Electric mixer

Wooden spoon

Baking sheet

Drinking glass

Cooling rack

This recipe makes thin, tasty, crispy cookies that hit the spot when you want something sweet and crunchy. Serve them with Bert and Ernie's Peary Delicious Applesauce (page 114) and a glass of milk, pack them to go, or give them as a gift.

1. Preheat the oven to 350°F.

2. 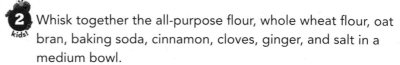 kids! Whisk together the all-purpose flour, whole wheat flour, oat bran, baking soda, cinnamon, cloves, ginger, and salt in a medium bowl.

3. In a large bowl, with an electric mixer on medium-high speed, beat together the sugar, oil, molasses, and egg until well blended. Stir in the flour mixture and mix well.

4. kids! Shape into 1-inch balls, roll them gently in sugar, and place the balls 2 inches apart on an ungreased baking sheet. Use the bottom of a drinking glass to gently flatten the cookies.

5. Bake for 10 minutes. Transfer the baking sheet to a rack to cool for 5 minutes. Transfer the cookies to the rack to cool completely.

NOTE: To make big, soft molasses cookies, substitute ¾ cup (1½ sticks) butter, softened, for the oil. In Step 3, beat the sugar and butter until light and fluffy, then add the molasses and egg and beat until blended. Roll the dough into 2-inch balls, place 2½ inches apart on the baking sheet, and bake for 11 to 12 minutes. (This makes 24 big cookies.)

VARIATION:
• Instead of cinnamon, cloves, and ginger, substitute the same total amount (2 teaspoons) of pumpkin pie spice.

VARIATION:
• Use whipped cream or pudding in place of the raspberry jam and chocolate to fill and top each cupcake.

TIP: Cupcakes are a "sometimes" food, perfect for special occasions and celebrations. These cupcakes substitute some "anytime" ingredients—such as oil instead of butter, low-fat yogurt to keep them moist and tender, and fresh raspberries for fruity fiber—to make them a little healthier.

Elmo loves surprises! And Elmo loves raspberries! Count the three raspberries on top of each cupcake you make—count them by 3s: 3, 6, 9.

ELMO'S Surprise! Chocolate-Raspberry Cupcakes

PREPARATION TIME: 15 MINUTES • BAKING TIME: 18 MINUTES • MAKES 12 CUPCAKES

Ingredients

1 cup all-purpose flour

½ cup sugar

⅓ cup unsweetened cocoa powder

1 teaspoon baking soda

⅛ teaspoon salt

2 eggs

½ cup low-fat plain yogurt

½ cup water

⅓ cup vegetable oil

½ teaspoon vanilla extract

¼ cup seedless raspberry jam

½ cup semisweet chocolate chips or mini chocolate chips

½ pint raspberries

Confectioner's sugar (optional)

Equipment

Measuring cups and spoons

12-cup muffin pan

Cupcake liners

Large bowl

Whisk

Medium bowl

Rubber spatula

Large spoon

Small knife

Small microwave-safe bowl

Cake tester/toothpick

Cooling rack

Table knife

The surprise is a sweet and drippy raspberry jam filling tucked inside each cupcake. Serve these light and airy cakes with a glass of milk and extra raspberries.

1. Preheat the oven to 350°F. Line 12 muffin pan cups with paper liners.

2. *kids!* Whisk together the flour, sugar, cocoa powder, baking soda, and salt in a large bowl.

3. *kids!* Whisk together the eggs and yogurt in a medium bowl. Whisk in the water, oil, and vanilla until smooth. Pour into the flour mixture, using a spatula to scrape the side of the bowl. Whisk just until blended.

4. Spoon the batter evenly into the lined muffin cups, filling each about two-thirds of the way full.

5. Bake for 18 minutes, or until a cake tester or toothpick inserted in the center of a cupcake comes out clean. Transfer the pan to a rack to cool for 10 minutes. Turn the cupcakes out onto the rack to cool completely.

6. When the cupcakes are cool, use a small knife to cut out a small cone shape from the top of each. Fill each hollow with 1 teaspoon jam, and replace the cone.

7. In a small microwave-safe bowl, microwave the chocolate chips for 20 to 30 seconds, until they start to melt. Stir until smooth. Spread about 1 teaspoon of melted chocolate over the center of each cupcake.

8. *kids!* Top each cupcake with 3 raspberries. If dusting with sugar, just before serving, pour a little confectioner's sugar in a wire mesh strainer and sprinkle lightly over cupcakes.

Ingredients

CAKE

1½ cups all-purpose flour

1½ teaspoons baking powder

½ teaspoon baking soda

¼ teaspoon salt

¼ cup (½ stick) butter, softened

¼ cup olive oil

1 cup sugar

2 eggs

½ cup (4 ounces) low-fat plain or flavored yogurt

1½ teaspoons vanilla extract

Chocolate or vanilla Cream Cheese Frosting (recipe follows)

Sweet Ricotta Filling (optional; recipe follows)

Chocolate Crumbs (optional; recipe follows)

Chopped drained fresh fruit (optional)

What's extra special about this cake is its flexibility—you can use it to make a single-layer cake, a dozen cupcakes, or 48 mini cupcakes. You can also double the recipe to make two 9-inch layers, a sheet cake, or twice as many cupcakes. And there are many different toppings you can try. Happy Birthday!

1. Preheat the oven to 350°F. Lightly oil and flour a 9-inch round cake pan, or line 12 muffin pan cups or 48 mini-muffin cups with paper liners.

2. kids! In a medium bowl, whisk together the flour, baking powder, baking soda, and salt until well blended.

3. In a large bowl, with an electric mixer on medium-high speed, beat the butter, oil, and sugar until well mixed. Beat in the eggs, one at a time.

4. With the mixer on low speed, beat in the flour mixture alternately with the yogurt, beginning and ending with the flour. Beat in the vanilla just until blended.

5. kids! With a rubber spatula, scrape the batter evenly into the prepared pan.

6. Bake until golden brown on top and a cake tester or toothpick inserted in the center comes out clean, 30 to 35 minutes for a cake layer, 18 minutes for cupcakes, or 10 minutes for mini cupcakes. Transfer the pan to a rack to cool completely.

7. When the cake layer is cool, run the tip of a knife around the side to loosen from the pan. Place a plate or another rack on top of the cake pan, invert, and turn the cake out. If making cupcakes, turn the cupcakes out onto the rack.

(Continued on page 124)

VARIATION:
- Sift confectioner's sugar or spread a little whipped cream over the top of a plain cake layer or cupcakes, and top with fresh fruit such as sliced peaches, strawberries, kiwis, or a combination of cut-up fruits and berries.

TIP: When you're serving up a sweet treat, start with just a small slice. With a rich dessert, that may be plenty. Serving it with colorful fresh fruit on a festive plate will add to its appeal!

Equipment

Measuring cups

Measuring spoons

9-inch round cake pan, 12-cup cupcake pan, or 48-cup mini cupcake pan

Cupcake liners (if making cupcakes)

Medium bowl

Whisk

Large bowl

Electric mixer

Rubber spatula

Cake tester/toothpick

Cooling rack

Table knife

8 kids! Frost the cake or cupcakes with the Cream Cheese Frosting. If you have made 2 cake layers, coat the first layer with the Sweet Ricotta Filling before placing the second cake layer on top. Top the cake or cupcakes with Chocolate Crumbs or chopped fresh fruit, if you like.

CREAM CHEESE FROSTING: In a large bowl, with an electric mixer on low speed, beat together 8 ounces reduced-fat cream cheese and 1½ cups confectioner's sugar. Beat in 1 teaspoon vanilla extract. (Makes about 1¼ cups frosting.) To make chocolate frosting, heat 2 ounces bittersweet or 70% dark chocolate pieces in a microwave-safe bowl in a microwave oven for 20 seconds. Stir, and then heat for 20 seconds longer, or until just melted. Stir this into the prepared Cream Cheese Frosting along with the vanilla. (Makes about 1½ cups frosting.) Double these frosting recipes, if you doubled the cake recipe, to make more frosting for multiple cake layers.

SWEET RICOTTA FILLING: In a blender or food processor, combine 1 cup part-skim ricotta cheese and ½ cup confectioner's sugar. Whirl for 30 seconds, or until very smooth. Transfer to a small bowl. Stir in ½ cup chopped strawberries, if you like.

CHOCOLATE CRUMBS: Whirl 2 ounces bittersweet or dark chocolate pieces or chips in a food processor until crumbs form.

When is *your* birthday? Find it on the calendar. How old will you be on your next birthday?

HAPPY BIRTHDAY!

When's your special day?

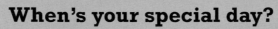

Say *feliz cumpleaños* to **Rosita** on December 7.

Telly's birthday is September 29.

Zoe's birthday is September 30.

Oscar the Grouch's birthday is June 1. Now scram!

Me celebrate with dee-licious cake on November 2. *Num num num.*

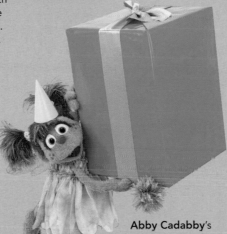

Abby Cadabby's birthday is October 21. Enchanting!

Elmo's birthday is February 3.

Ernie's special day is January 28.

His buddy **Bert** celebrates on July 26.

Big Bird's big day is March 20.

Grover's birthday is October 14.

Count von Count's birthday is October 9.

Together Time

Cooking together is just one way to learn and have fun at mealtimes. Here are some others:

ABC fun

Together, look again at the ABCs of Healthy Food on page 10.

• Help your child categorize the food photos by food groups. Which ones are fruits? Which are vegetables? Which are dairy and protein?

• Provide materials such as crayons, markers, and colored pencils, as well as drawing paper. Write the letters of your child's name across the top and invite him to draw pictures of foods that start with those letters.

• Ask your child which of the featured foods she'd like to try using for a breakfast meal. Which ones would she prefer for lunch or dinner? Add a few of them to your next grocery list!

Table fun

As much as possible, try to sit down for meals together. It's a great way to strengthen family bonds and to grow vocabulary.

• Challenge your child—and everyone at the table—to think of words that describe the foods on the table. For example, spaghetti with tomato sauce could be spicy, messy, slurpy, and so on. This is a great vocabulary builder.

• Build a funny conversation around food! Take turns contributing ideas for the "yuckiest pizza topping," for instance. You can start by saying, "Oscar likes sardines and rotten bananas on his pizza."

• Play this table game to encourage looking for the best in people. Designate one member of the family the "honoree." Go around the table asking everyone to say one nice thing about that person. Then extend the game! What's the best thing about Cookie Monster? How about Slimey the Worm?

• Talk about where foods on the table came from, before they got to the market. Which ones grew on trees? Which grew under the ground, or came from the ocean? It's great for kids to know all the things (and people) that go into getting food onto their table.

• Ask each person: What was the best thing that happened to you today? Maybe the answer will be "helping to make dinner," or even "sitting together right now!"

Murray's big words: chewy scrumptious salty tangy crunchy

Index

Page numbers in *italics* indicate illustrations